·VIOLINS

AND OTHER

STRINGED INSTRUMENTS

HOW TO MAKE THEM

WITH NUMEROUS ENGRAVINGS AND DIAGRAMS

EDITED BY

PAUL N. HASLUCK

EDITOR OF "WORK" AND "BUILDING WORLD"
AUTHOR OF "HANDYBOOKS FOR HANDICRAFTS," ETC. ETC.

1907

British Library Cataloguing-in-Publication Data
A catalogue record for this book is available from the
British Library

Paul Nooncree Hasluck

Paul Nooncree Hasluck was born in April 1854, in South Australia. The third son of Lewis Hasluck, of Perth, the family moved to the UK when Hasluck was still young. He subsequently lived in Herne Bay (Kent), before moving to 120 Victoria Street, London, later in life. Hasluck was the secretary of the 'Institution of Sanitary Engineers' – an organisation dedicated to promoting knowledge of, and development in the field of urban sanitation. Hasluck was also the editor of several magazines and volumes over his lifetime, including *Work Handbooks*, and *Building World*. He was an eminently knowledgeable and talented engineer, and wrote many practical books. These included such titles as; *Lathe-Work: A Practical Treatise on the Tools employed in the Art of Turning* (1881), *The Watch-Jobber's Handy Book* (1887), *Screw-Threads, and Methods of Producing Them* (1887), and an eight volume series on *The Automobile* as well as a staggering eighteen volumes of *Mechanics Manuals*.

In his personal life, Hasluck married in 1883, to 'Florence' – and the two enjoyed a happy marriage, though his wife unfortunately died young, in 1916. Hasluck himself died on 7th May, 1931, aged seventy-seven.

A History of the Violin

The violin, also known as a fiddle, is a string instrument, usually with four strings tuned in perfect fifths. It is the smallest, highest-pitched member of the violin family of string instruments, which also includes the viola, the cello and the double bass. The violinist produces sound by drawing a bow across one or more strings (which may be stopped by the fingers of the other hand to produce a full range of pitches), by plucking the strings (with either hand), or by a variety of other techniques. The violin is played by musicians in a wide variety of musical genres, including such diverse styles as baroque, classical, jazz, folk and rock and roll.

The violin, while it has ancient origins, acquired most of its modern characteristics in 16th-century Italy, with some further modifications occurring in the 18th and 19th centuries. Violinists and collectors particularly prize the instruments made by the Gasparo da Salò, Giovanni Paolo Maggini, Stradivari, Guarneri and Amati families from the 16th to the 18th century in Brescia and Cremona and by Jacob Stainer in Austria. A person who makes or repairs violins is called a luthier, and will almost always work with wood – utilising gut, perlon or steel to string the instrument.

The history of the violin is long and varied; and the earliest stringed instruments were mostly plucked (e.g. the Greek lyre). Bowed instruments may have originated in the equestrian cultures of Central Asia – for instance the 'Tanbur' of Uzbekistan or the 'Kobyz'; an ancient Turkic string instrument. Such two-string upright fiddles were strung with horsehair and played with horsehair bows; they often features a carved horses head at the end of the neck too. The violins, violas and cellos we play today, and whose bows are still strung with horsehair are a legacy of these nomadic peoples.

It is believed that these instruments eventually spread to China, India, the Byzantine Empire and the Middle East, where they developed into instruments such as the erhu in China, the rebab in the Middle East, the lyra in the Byzantine Empire and the esraj in India. The modern European violin as we know it evolved from the Middle Eastern stringed instruments, and one of the earliest explicit descriptions of this musical device, including its tuning was made in France in the sixteenth century. This was a book entitled *Epitome Musical*, by Jambe de Fer, published in Lyon in 1556 – and helped popularise the instrument all over Europe. Several further significant changes occurred in violin construction in the eighteenth century – making it closer to our current instrument. These primarily involved a longer neck at a slightly different angle, as well as a heavier bass bar.

The oldest documented violin to have four strings, like the modern variant, is supposed to have been constructed in 1555 by Andrea Amati. However in the 1510s (some fifty years before the flourishing activity of Andrea Amati), there were sevedn 'lireri', or makers of bowed instruments, including proto-violins listed in the city. The violin was quickly hailed by nobility and street players alike, illustrated by the fact that the French king Charles IX ordered Amati to construct twenty-four violins for him in 1560. One of these instruments, now called the *Charles IX,* is the oldest surviving violin. The *finest* Renaissance carved and decorated violin in the world is the Gasparo da Salò (c. 1574), owned by Ferdinand II, Archduke of Austria and later, from 1841, by the Norweigian virtuoso Ole Bull. Bull used it for forty years, during which he became famed for his powerful and beautiful tone – it is now kept in the Vestlandske Kustindustrimuseum in Begen (Norway). Another famous violin, 'Le Messie' (also known as the 'Salabue'), made in 1716 is now located in the Ashmolean Museum of Oxford, England.

To this day, instruments from the so-called Golden Age of violin making, especially those made by Stradivari, Guarneri del Gesù and Montagnana are the most sought-after instruments by both collectors and performers. The current record amount paid for a Stradivari violin is £9.8 million (US$15.9 million), when the instrument known as the Lady Blunt was sold by Tarisio Auctions in an online auction on June 20, 2011. We hope the reader is inspired by this book to find out more about the intriguing and complex history of this wonderful instrument.

PREFACE.

THIS Handbook contains, in form convenient for
everyday use, a comprehensive digest of the knowledge
of making Violins and other Stringed Instruments,
scattered over more than forty thousand columns of
WORK—one of the weekly journals it is my fortune
to edit—and supplies concise information on the details
of the subjects of which it treats.

In preparing for publication in book form the mass
of relevant matter contained in the volumes of WORK,
much had to be arranged anew, altered, and largely
rewritten. From these causes it is difficult to dis-
tinguish the writings of individuals for acknowledg-
ment, but it may be said that contributions from the
pens of Mr. David McSkimming and Mr. Robert Ford
are incorporated in this work.

Readers who may desire additional information
respecting special details of the matters dealt with in
this Handbook, or instructions on kindred subjects,
should address a question to The Editor, WORK, La
Belle Sauvage, London, E.C., so that it may be
answered in the columns of that journal.

P. N. HASLUCK.

La Belle Sauvage, London,
January, 1906.

CONTENTS.

CHAPTER   PAGE

I.—Materials and Tools for Violin Making .   9

II.—Making Violin Moulds 30

III.—Violin Making 41

IV.—Varnishing and Finishing Violins . . 64

V.—Double Bass Violin, and a Violoncello . 71

VI.—Japanese One-String Violins . . 77

VII.—Mandoline Making 82

VIII.—Guitar Making 92

IX.—Banjo Making   , ... 99

X.—Zither Making 117

XI.—Dulcimer Making 141

Index 159

LIST OF ILLUSTRATIONS.

FIG.   PAGE

1.—Finished Violin . 11
2.—Section of Sycamore or Pine cut on the quarter . . . 11
3.—Piece marked for Sawing down . 11
4.—Jointed Piece for Violin Belly . . 11
5.—Apparatus for Bending Violin Ribs . 12
6-9.—Bending Irons 13, 14
10, 11.—Iron Cramps . 15
12, 13.—Cramps for Fixing Back and Belly to Ribs . . . 15
14.—Cramp for Fixing Linings . . . 15
15.—Hand-screws . . 16
16.—Wood-carver's Screw . 16
17.—Spring Dividers . 16
18.—Spring Callipers . 16
19.—Steel Compasses . 16
20.—Square . . . 16
21.—Cutting Gauge . 17
22.—Sweeps or Curves of Gouges . . . 17
23, 24. — Thicknessing Gauges . . . 18
25.—Thicknessing Callipers . . . 19
26.—Register Gauge . 19
27.—Bearing or Fulcrum of Callipers . 19
28, 29. — Elevations of Thicknessing Appliance . . 20
30.—Boxwood Gauge . 20
31.—Guide . . . 20
32-35.—Thumb Planes 23, 24
36, 37.—Plane Pattern . 25
38, 39.—Core-box . 25
40.—Lever Wedge . 25
41.—Steel Scrapers . 26
42-44.—Purfling Gauges 27, 28
45, 46.—Cutter of Purfling Gauge . . 28
47.—Purfling Gauge . 29
48.—Purfling Knife . 29
49.—Purfling Picker . 29
50.—Outside Mould . 30
51.—Inside Mould . 31
52.—Half of Outside Mould 34
53, 54.—Outside and Inside Pattern . . 38

FIG.   PAGE

55.—Mould Block ready for Sawing Out . 39
56.—Stages in Bending Waist Ribs . . 43
57.—Diagram showing Directions for Cutting Corners . . 47
58.—Back with Edge reduced ready for Purfling . . . 47
59.—Pattern for Arching Lengthwise . . 47
60.—Pattern for Arching across Waist . . 47
61.—Diagram showing Method of Purfling Waists and Cutting Mitres . . . 49
62.—Set of Ribs with Linings . . . 51
63.—Blocks for Hollowing 53
64.—Diagram showing Thickness of Violin Back . . . 54
65.—Diagram showing Thickness of Violin Belly . . . 55
66.—Pattern for Sound Hole . . . 57
67.—Bass-bar . . . 57
68.—Section of Block for Making Neck and Scroll . . . 59
69.—Pattern for Making Violin Neck and Scroll . . . 59
70.—Outline of Head Back 59
71.—Front Outline of Head 60
72.—Pattern of Neck . 61
73.—Cutting Bevel for Shoulder . . . 61
74, 75.—Front and Side Views of Double Bass Violin . . 72
76.—Diagram showing Position of Bass-bar, Sound-holes, etc. . 73
77, 78.—Bass-bar for Violoncello . . . 76
79, 80.—Japanese Violin . 78
81.—Half-size Detail of Body . . . 80
82-84.—Japanese Violin Handle . . . 80

FIG.		PAGE
85, 86.—Method of Fitting Machine Head	.	80
87, 88.—Button for Securing String	. .	81
89, 90.—Knee Caps	. .	81
91, 92.—Setting out Handle of Flat-backed Mandoline	.	83
93.—Inside Mould for Flat-backed Mandoline	.	84
94, 95.—Partition for Flat-backed Mandoline		85
96.—Fixing Handle and Back of Mandoline		86
97.—Strengthening Blocks on Rim of Mandoline	. .	86
98.—Position of Sound Holes and Bridge on Mandoline	. .	87
99.—Mandoline Bridge	.	87
100-102. — Tail-piece for Mandoline	.	88
103.—American Mandoline with Machine Head		89
104.—Outside Mould for American Mandoline	. .	90
105.—Spanish Guitar	.	92
106.—Andalusian Guitar	.	94
107.—French Guitar	.	94
108.—American Guitar	.	95
109.—Spanish Lyre-guitar		95
110.—Inside Mould for Guitar	. .	96
111.—Guitar Bridge, showing Method of Fastening Strings		97
112, 113.—Handle of Banjo		100
114.—Ivory Slip	. .	101
115.—Peg	. . .	101
116, 117.—Wood Clamp for Making Banjo	.	101
118.—Banjo Bowl	. .	102
119.—Screw for Banjo Handle	. .	102
120-122.—Clamping Bracket		102
123, 124.—Clamping Screw and Nut	. .	103
125.—Bracket	.	104
126.—Tail-piece of Banjo	.	104
127.—Banjo Bridge	.	104
128, 129.—Handle of Piccolo Banjo	.	105
130.—Peg	. .	107
131.—Bowl	. . .	107
132.—Taper Screw	.	108
133.—Section of Banjo Ring	. .	108
134-136.—Clamp and Screw		109
137.—Clamping Screw for Parchment	.	109
138.—Clamp Screw for Tail-piece	.	109

FIG.		PAGE
139.—Tail-piece of Banjo		110
140.—Banjo Bridge	. .	110
141.—Elégie Zither	.	117
142.—Concert Zither	.	118
143.—Under Side of Zither Belly	. .	119
144.—Getting out Top and Bottom Blocks	.	120
145.—Diagonal Stay	.	121
146.—Zither in Mould and Cramps	. .	122
147.—Long Stay	. .	123
148.—Upper Block and Bridge, with Wrest-pins, etc.	. .	124
149.—Lower End of Zither		125
150.—Stuttgart Method of Tuning Zithers	.	130
151.—Viennese Method of Tuning Zither	.	131
152.—Arion Zither	.	134
153, 154.—Harp Zithers	134, 135
155.—Streich or Bow Zither	. .	135
156.—Philomela Zither or Zither-viola	.	136
157.—Prince of Wales' Harp	. .	138
158.—Tongue of Material to form Plectrum	.	140
159.—Ring or Plectrum	.	140
160.—Concert Ring or Plectrum	. .	140
161.—Cutting Wrest-pin and Hitch-pin Blocks	.	142
162.—Section of Block with Groove	.	143
163.—Section of Block with Fillet for Dulcimer Belly	.	143
164.—Marking off Corners	144
165.—Fitting Blocks into Angles of Back	.	145
166.—Inner Bridges	.	146
167.—Shell of Dulcimer	.	147
168.—Front of Dulcimer with Facing on	.	148
169.—Full-size Wrest-pin	.	148
170.—Setting out Dulcimer Hitch-pin Block	.	149
171.—Full-size Bridge for Dulcimer	. .	150
172.—Dulcimer Stand	.	151
173.—Making Moulding round Dulcimer Belly	. .	152
174.—Eye for Dulcimer String	. .	153
175.—Properly Wound Pin	155
176.—Badly Wound Pin	.	155
177.—Scale and Approximate Position of Bridge	. . .	157

VIOLINS

STRINGED INSTRUMENTS.

—•◦•—

CHAPTER I.

MATERIALS AND TOOLS FOR VIOLIN-MAKING.

THE early chapters of a handbook on the making of stringed musical instruments must almost of necessity be devoted to the violin, which takes pre-eminence, of course, of all other instruments of its class. While it is not the present purpose to trace the history of the violin, it must yet be said that the instruments which came from the workshops of the Cremonese masters, some 300 years ago, have not been surpassed, probably not even equalled, by any which have since been made. Although the science of acoustics has kept pace with other branches of knowledge, the efforts of the great masters have not been improved upon, and the best results in violin making have been obtained by following as closely as possible the lines laid down by the Cremonese makers during the seventeenth century. Though opinions differ as to the relative merits of the various outlines and models, it will be taken for granted here that the outline, measurements, and f holes of the "Stradivarius" are the best (see Fig. 1), and accordingly the necessary diagrams and patterns used in making an instrument of this class will be given, together with all needful instructions on the methods of using tools and materials.

The very best material is a necessity in making a good violin. Notwithstanding all the arguments in

favour of artificially prepared wood, there is no doubt
that naturally seasoned wood is by far the best, and
most likely to improve with age and use.

For the belly is required a **V** or wedge-shaped block
of clean, even-grained Swiss pine, 15 in. long by about
5 in. broad, 2 in. thick at one edge, and tapering to
about ¾ in. at the other. This block should be cut on
the quarter shown in Fig. 2 ; Fig. 3 shows the piece
marked for sawing down. This method gives the reeds
or veins, which are portions of the concentric rings,
running vertically through the wood in the direction of
its thickness. A like result is obtained by using the
middle board, but in this case the two halves of the
back or belly would not necessarily correspond in grain
or in figure ; and as work is to be done with a half
pattern, from a centre line, it is better to have the wood
cut as in Fig. 3. It is only when cut on the "quarter"
that pine gives the beautiful mottled and silky appearance known as "flower." The table from which the
belly is to be made should, when jointed and planed
true (as in Fig. 4), be ⅜ in. thick at the ridge. Care
should be taken when selecting this wedge to see that it
has been "riven" or split, not sawn, so that the fibres
have run in their natural direction.

. The back is generally of sycamore, cut also on the
quarter ; the stripes or bars in sycamore show at their
best only when cut in this way. These strong bars or
waves are termed the "figure." The piece for the back
should be 15 in. long, 1¾ in. thick at one edge, and about
⅝ in. at the other. Good back wood is very valuable,
and the pieces are therefore cut so fine that there is
very little margin for waste.

The "ribs," or sides, are of sycamore, and may easily
be purchased in strips, cut for the purpose, 15 or 16 in.
long, by 1⅔ in. broad, and about $\frac{1}{12}$ in. thick. They
should not require much cleaning up before being ready
for use.

The neck is cut from a block of sycamore, 10½ in.
long, 2 in. broad, and 2½ in. deep, and the 2 in. side

should be that nearest the tree. The carving of the scroll is one of the most difficult operations in making a violin throughout ; and as it either greatly beautifies or entirely spoils the appearance of the whole instrument,

Fig. 1.—Finished Violin.

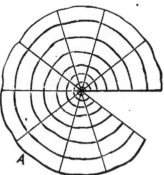

Fig. 2.—Section of Sycamore or Pine cut on the quarter.

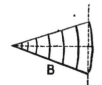

Fig. 3.—Piece marked for Sawing Down.

Fig. 4.—Jointed Piece for Violin Belly.

it is better in the generality of cases to buy a neck with the scroll already cut.

The bass-bar is a most important part of a violin, and on its dimensions and position depend to a large extent the tone of the lower strings. It is made of even-grained Swiss pine, and in the rough should measure 11 in. long by ¼ in. thick and 1 in. deep, the reeds running vertically through its depth and parallel with the whole length of the bar. It should be placed parallel with the joint of the belly, under the left foot of the bridge.

The sound-post is a round piece of fine-grained Swiss pine, ¼ in. diameter, and about $2\frac{3}{16}$ in. long. Its position varies in nearly every instrument, but is usually just behind the right foot of the bridge. It should be just long enough to stand firmly before the

Fig. 5.—Apparatus for Bending Violin Ribs.

violin is strung, and the grain should cross that of the belly.

The blocks should be made of nice clean pine, 1 in. thick, from the middle board, if possible, as they will then be on the quarter, and will cut much cleaner. The grain runs vertically from back to belly. They afford support to the neck and end pin, hold the ribs together at the corners, and strengthen the fiddle generally.

The twelve pieces of lining are put in to strengthen the ribs, and to give a greater gluing surface for attaching back and belly. They may be made from pine or sycamore, and are $\frac{1}{18}$ in. thick and ¼ in. broad ; sycamore is not so liable to splinter when necessity arises to have either the back or the belly removed.

Purfling may be bought from violin makers or dealers at about 1d. per foot, and is generally made of two thin strips of wood, dyed black, with a strip of white wood between, the whole being about $\frac{1}{16}$ in. thick and $\frac{1}{12}$ in. deep. Some of the great makers used whalebone for making the black parts of purfling.

Next to the wood, the glue used is a very important material. Good glue of the ordinary kind, as transparent

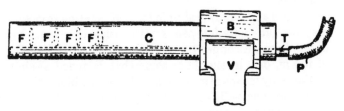

Fig. 6.—Simple Form of Bending Iron.

and light in colour as possible, is all that is required, and it must not be overcooked. If, however, a damp-proof glue is preferred, dissolve 1 lb. of ordinary glue in $\frac{1}{2}$ gal. of skim milk ; or make the glue with water in the ordinary way, and to every 30 or 40 parts of glue add 1 part of bichromate of potash. The last-named mixture must be made and kept in the dark, as the action of light makes it insoluble in water.

In addition to the ordinary tools which are found in

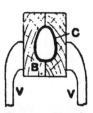

Fig. 7.—Simple Form of Bend-ing Iron.

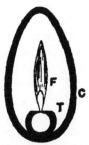

Fig. 8.—Section of Bending Iron.

any joiner's shop, such as smoothing plane, trying plane, saws, chisels, and the like, some special tools are necessary. They can be bought from certain firms, but most of the tools can be easily and cheaply made at home.

An apparatus for bending violin ribs is shown by
Fig. 5. It is a piece of ¾ in. iron pipe, cut open all the
length, and is heated by a row of gas jets underneath.
The tube is fixed in an iron vice, and the gas heater is
suspended from it by wires passing round each end of
the tube.

Figs. 6 and 7 show a simple form of bending iron which
may be made for a few pence. It consists of a 9 in. length
of solid-drawn copper tube C, ¾ in. in external diameter;
of it 5 in. or 6 in. should be somewhat flattened, as shown
at Fig. 8, by means of a wooden mallet and a block of wood.
The other end is fitted between two hollowed blocks of
wood B (Fig. 7), and gripped in the vice V, or in a large
handscrew which may be fastened in the lug of the bench,

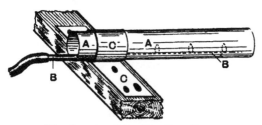

Fig. 9.—Another Bending Iron.

the copper tube lying horizontally and projecting towards
the workman. Inside the bottom of the copper tube
lies a 9 in. length of brass tube T, ¼ in. in external
diameter. The top edge of the brass tube is flattened by
filing till the metal is thin enough to allow holes to be
punched with a needle. One end of this tube is staved
up or soldered gas-tight, and an indiarubber connection
P made to a gas tap from the other. Four or five
minute jets F are thus provided for heating up the
copper tube, and the heat can be regulated to a nicety.

A similar bending device to that shown by Figs. 6 and
7 is illustrated by Fig. 9, but instead of being enclosed
in a wooden block, it is fixed by means of a brass or iron
clip C to a short piece of hard wood, and the wood is
gripped in a vice, or screwed down to the work bench

while using.   The ⅜ in. brass tube just lies along the
bottom of the larger tube, both ends of which are kept
open.   In Fig. 9, A is the outer tube and B the brass
gas-tube.

Another excellent bending iron can be made as

Fig. 10.

Fig. 11.

Figs. 10 and 11.—Iron Cramps.

follows : Get a 6 in. length of hydraulic iron tube 1 in.
external diameter, with a flange screwed on one end ;
any plumber would supply this for a few pence.   The
flange is gripped in a table vice, leaving the tube projecting horizontally towards the worker.   Behind it is
rigged up a short length of brass tube, ⅜ in., into which
is fixed one of those burners usually placed on stairs,
giving a long, straight, pointed flame.   This is connected
to the gas by an indiarubber tube, and the flame directed
into the centre of the iron tube from behind.   The heat

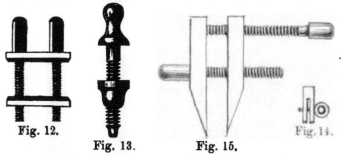

Fig. 12.

Fig. 13.   Fig. 15.

Fig. 14.

Figs. 12 and 13.—Cramps for Fixing Back and Belly to Ribs.
Fig. 14.—Cramp for Fixing Linings.   Fig. 15.—Hand-Screws.

can be regulated to a nicety, and kept at the proper
temperature all the time.

Two forms of iron cramps are shown by Figs. 10 and
11 ; six of the smaller are required for fixing the ribs on
the mould.   Fig. 12 shows a cramp which is used in

fixing the back and belly to the ribs, but a superior cramp is illustrated by Fig. 13 ; this is lined with cork on both the inner sides, and cannot possibly injure the most delicate instrument. The small cramp (Fig. 14) is

Fig. 16.—Wood-carver's Screw.

used for fixing linings in the waists ; the other linings do not need cramps.

Hand screws (Fig. 15) are often wanted ; two or three sizes should always be at hand.

A wood-carver's screw (Fig. 16) is also very useful. Its point is to be firmly screwed into a carving block, and the stem passed through a hole in the bench, underneath which the wing nut is screwed on the stem.   The

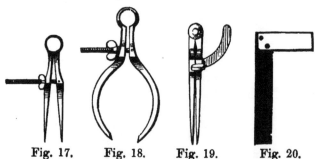

Fig. 17.   Fig. 18.   Fig. 19.   Fig. 20.

Fig. 17.—Spring Dividers.   Fig. 18.—Spring Callipers.
Fig. 19.—Steel Compasses. Fig. 20.—Square

carving block may be turned in any position, and, by tightening the nut previously loosened, instantly made fast again.

Spring dividers (Fig. 17), which are used for measuring distances very finely. The spring callipers (Fig. 18), will be very useful, especially when finishing the neck. A pair of strong steel compasses (Fig. 19) must be

Fig. 21.—Cutting Gauge.

obtained. Do not use the dividers for any purpose for which the compasses are intended.

A small square (Fig. 20) is in frequent requisition for such purposes as squaring the rib ends, testing the truth of blocks, etc.

A cutting gauge (Fig. 21) is useful for reducing the edges of back and belly to their proper thickness.

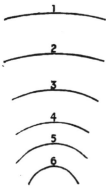

Fig. 22.—Sweeps or Curves of Gouges.

A set of gouges must be obtained; tools corresponding to the "sweeps," or curves, given in Fig. 22, will be sufficient, but a fiddle maker, it may be said, cannot have too many kinds of gouges. Some workers believe

B

however, that a rounded spokeshave is a better tool for hollowing out than the gouge.

The thicknessing gauge, or automatic measurer, is one of the most important tools in a violin-maker's kit. The gauge shown by Fig. 23 was invented by

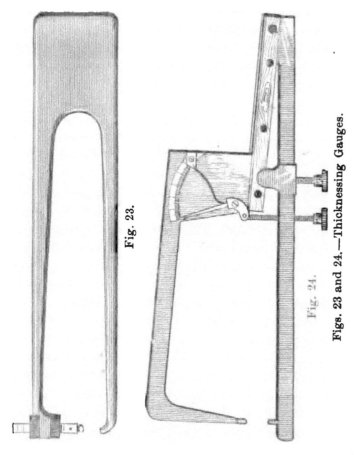

Fig. 23.

Fig. 24.

Figs. 23 and 24.—Thicknessing Gauges.

Mr. William Tarr a great many years ago. It is extremely simple in its action, gives the most accurate measurements, and is not likely to get out of order. The small point of the gauge being held lightly underneath the back or belly, the ivory rule, whose point traverses the surface, shows it at a glance in thirty-seconds of an inch. A still more convenient gauge is Hill's, shown by Fig. 24; the thickness gauged is shown by the pointer on the sector.

Another kind of thicknessing gauge or callipers can

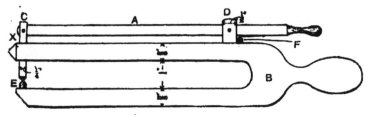

Fig. 25.—Thicknessing Callipers.

be made of hard wood, and is shown complete by Fig. 25. The part A is 10¾ in. long by ⅜ in. by ¼ in.; B is 13 in. long by 2¼ in. by ½ in.; E is a round pin ¼ in. high, rounded to a point which must meet the register gauge c (shown separately in Fig. 26). Whatever thickness is between those points will be registered at the point marked x in Fig. 25. F is a spring which enables the register gauge, c, to rise or fall and register the exact thickness as it is drawn over the back or belly of the violin to be measured. A hole ¼ in. square must be made through the upper arm of B to admit the

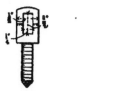

Fig. 26.—Register   Fig. 27.—Bearing or Fulcrum
Gauge.   of Callipers.

register, c. Fig. 27 is an enlarged view of the bearing or fulcrum D (Fig. 25).

Regular thicknessing is an essential in the production of a high-grade violin. The work necessary for this is most arduous, consisting of endless careful gouging and

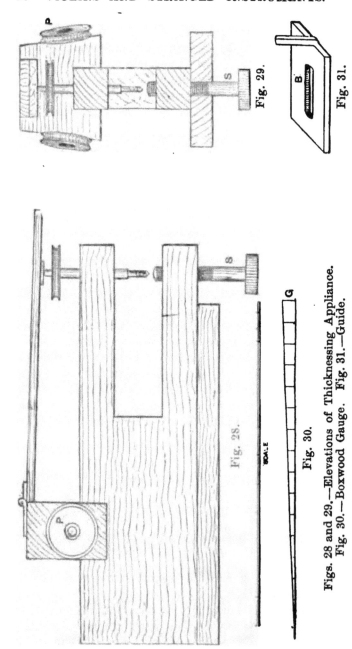

Figs. 28 and 29.—Elevations of Thicknessing Appliance.
Fig. 30.—Boxwood Gauge.   Fig. 31.—Guide.

callipering, during which a careless stroke with the tool
or an error in reading the callipers may spoil all the
results of the labour. To obviate these objections the
thickening appliance shown in Figs. 28 and 29 has been
devised. It reduces enormously the time spent in
thicknessing the plates, and at the same time ensures
accuracy. The motive power may be a lathe treadle
and fly-wheel, in which case the appliance is bolted
down to the lathe bed in the position occupied by the
mandrel head, which is temporarily removed, the appliance being allowed to hang over the bed to the left so
as to leave the regulating screw free. An old sewing-
machine stand may be used, the flywheel lying along
instead of across the stand, thus allowing the appliance
to be placed with the drill towards the operator, and
hanging a few inches over the front of the table. A
$\frac{3}{16}$-in. gut band is used as a driving belt, with hook and
eye fastenings as used on lathes. The two guide pulleys
P (Figs. 28 and 29) are grooved, and are 1 in. in
diameter ; they may be got ready bored at the iron-
monger's for a few pence, and are set at such an angle
as to be in a line with the rim of the flywheel, the
axles being common screw nails. The block which
carries the pulleys also supports a hinged lever used for
pressing down the drill, the lever having a small metal
plate screwed on it to bear on the top end of the drill.
The drill is made from a piece of drill steel 4 in. long
and about $\frac{5}{32}$ in. thick, as sold by watchmakers'
furnishers, and on it a pulley, the same as the guide
pulleys, is driven tight about $\frac{1}{4}$ in. from the top end, the
cutting point being formed on the other end. Heat and
then hammer flat about 1 in. of the end, which may
then be twisted with pliers and filed into a diamond
point with rather sharp cutting edges, and tempered to
a straw colour, the top edge of the flame of an ordinary
bat's-wing gas burner being used for heating. The drill
is journalled in a 2-in. length of brass tubing driven
tightly into the upper wooden arm. The positions of
the guide pulleys and the driven pulley are so arranged

that the drill will rise when the pressure on the lever is
released. The brass regulating screw s (Figs. 28 and 29)
is 3 in. long and $\frac{3}{8}$ in. in diameter, screwed thirty-six
threads to the inch, with a milled head. The hole to
receive it is bored a tight fit, and the screw is simply
allowed to make its own thread in the hard wood of the
lower arm, the top end of the screw being rounded to
prevent its marking the finished surface of the plate as
it is moved about on it.

The boxwood gauge of the thicknessing appliance (see
Fig. 30) may be divided either into 64ths or 100ths of an
inch. A simple way to do this is to plane up a piece of
boxwood 8 in. long and $\frac{5}{16}$ in. thick by about $\frac{3}{8}$ in.,
perfectly straight on one of the broad sides. Then,
with thin glue, fasten it to a piece of $\frac{3}{8}$-in. wood of the
same length, and with a piece of tissue paper between
them, keeping the ends flush. The boxwood is then
planed down from exactly $\frac{1}{4}$ in. thick at one end to a
knife edge at the other, and a table knife inserted
between the two thicknesses will split the tissue paper
and separate them, when the adhering paper may be
sponged off. If the wood is then divided into sixteen
parts in the length, each division will represent $\frac{1}{64}$ in. of
an increase in thickness.

In making a belly with this appliance, after the outside
of the table has been finished to gauge, the lines of equal
thickness are marked in pencil on the inside, and a row
of holes about $\frac{1}{2}$ in. apart drilled along each line to the
exact depth required, intermediate lines of intermediate
thicknesses being added, if more perfect gradation is
desired. Longitudinal and cross sections showing the
curves of thickness can be made, and from them can be
got the lines of equal thickness, putting in plenty of
lines to give a great number of guiding points. The
depth to which the drill will cut is regulated by inserting
the wedge-shaped gauge to the required division between
the drill and the screw gauge, and screwing the latter up
until the wedge gauge just touches both at the desired
mark. When all the points have been drilled, no further

gauging will be required. All that is necessary is to start with the gouge, or, better still, a bent spokeshave, and cut fearlessly away until the bottoms of the holes are nearly reached, leaving them about $\frac{1}{16}$ in. in diameter meantime. The small round-soled hand plane (described later) may then be used till there is just a trace of the point of the drill remaining; then sandpaper on a rounded cork pad will do the rest. It is useful also, when getting the preliminary scoop round the edges, to add the decided raised edge beyond the purfling,

Fig. 32.—Thumb Plane.

which adds both to the strength and character of the fiddle. For this purpose use the guide or fence B (Fig. 31). This is simply a piece of sheet brass with a slot to allow of adjustment, one end being turned up, reduced to $\frac{1}{8}$ in. broad, and rounded to enable it to fit into the curves of the inner bouts.

Round steel shell bits are used by some violin makers for cutting the circular extremities of the sound holes, the bits having diameters of $\frac{1}{4}$ in. and $\frac{5}{16}$in. respectively. These holes may also be bored with centre-bits of the sizes mentioned ; but great care must be taken not to use too much pressure, as the sound holes lose much of their beauty if the sharp corners be broken off.

A slightly tapered shell-bit for boring the peg holes in the handle will also be wanted.

Thumb planes (Fig. 32) consist of a stock or body, blade, and wedge. The stock is cast in gun-metal or common brass. By way of example, the making of a medium size plane (1½ in. long) will be described. The shapes of the sole are peculiar ; some are flat in cross-section, but curve fore and aft ; others may be round both ways, like the ball of the thumb. The instructions about to be given for making these planes apply to any shape, but particularly to that shown in Figs 33 to 35,

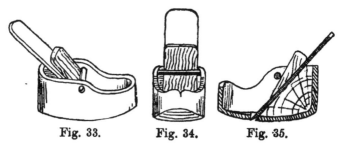

Fig. 33.   Fig. 34.   Fig. 35.

Figs. 33 and 34.—Side and Front Views of Thumb Planes.
Fig. 35.—Cross Section of Thumb Plane.

and the maker should use such patterns of sole as are found most useful.

For the foundry pattern of the plane use a piece of hard wood 1½ in. by ⅞ in. by ⅞ in. Draw a centre line right round the block, as in Figs. 36 and 37, and set out the shape. Then pare it down with a sharp chisel. Nail on a print for the core, $\frac{3}{32}$ in. smaller all round than the body of the plane, and slightly tapered. Set out the front of the plane as in Fig. 36, and cut down from the edge of the print. Draw a line ⅛ in. from the bottom, and give the bottom the shape desired, the illustrations giving a general idea of what is useful. The core-box, shown generally in Fig. 38 and in section at Fig. 39, is made in halves, dowelled loosely together. The recess for the core is made to the same shape and diameters as the top of the print. The depth of the core is measured

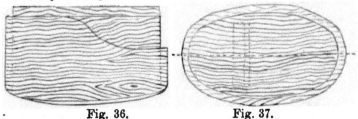

Fig. 36.   Fig. 37.

Figs. 36 and 37.—Elevation and Plan of Plane Pattern.

from the top of the print, care being taken to leave enough metal on the bottom for filing smooth and polishing. The core-box will be more easily made if each half is built in two pieces, this method enabling the maker to cut the sides squarer than if the half were in one. If a flat bottom inside is required for a flat-soled

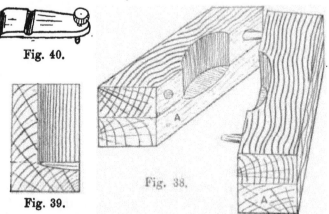

Fig. 40.

Fig. 39.

Fig. 38.—General View of Core-box. Fig. 39.—Section of Core-box. Fig. 40.—Lever Wedge.

plane the piece A would not be necessary. Give both the pattern and inside of the core-box two or three coats of spirit varnish, sandpapering between each coat.

Having got the castings from the founder, first file up
the sides square, then the top edges ; next drive a short
piece of wood into the plane, and, holding this in the
vice, file the bottom smooth and even ; polish the plane
all over, and burnish it. Next procure a piece of steel
wire, about ⅛ in. diameter and a little longer than the
width of the plane. Mark off, and drill two holes for
the same, 1⅜ in. from the fore end of the plane and ₁₆ in.
from the top edge. This pin should require driving in
with a light hammer. Mark off the mouth of the plane,
as denoted by dotted lines in Fig. 37, and by section in
Fig. 35, ½ in. from the front, ₁₆ in. wide, and ⅛ in. bare
across. Drill a hole at each end of the mouth, and cut
out to the lines with a fretsaw. Clean out the mouth

Fig. 41.—Steel Scrapers.

with a ward file, bevelling the back of the mouth as
shown, so that the cutter will have a good bearing. For
the cutter a piece of steel, ₁₆ in. thick, ₁₆ in. wide, and
2½ in. long, is required. Round the cutting edge to suit
the curve of the sole, and file three or five fine notches
on the lower side of the edge of the iron. These notches
are best made with the sharp edge of a smooth half-
round file. Temper this cutter to a straw colour. Now
knock the pin home, and lightly rivet ; fit a piece of
wood for the iron to lie on, put the iron in, and see that
it beds fair. Finish by cutting a hardwood wedge to
hold the iron in place.

A lever wedge of gun-metal or steel, as shown at
Fig. 40, is often seen in small planes (see the full size
view of a plane given by Fig. 32). To put it in
position, slip it in the plane, then put in the iron. A

turn or two of the screw will hold all tight. The wooden wedge, however, is simple, and holds perfectly.

A fine-toothed plane, such as cabinet makers use for veneering, is frequently required, more especially for sycamore, which is strong in " figure."

Oilstones will be required for sharpening gouges, plane irons, and chisels.

Steel scrapers (see Fig. 41) are wanted ; these have one flat edge and three different round ones. The edges should be ground square across, the scraper placed edgeways in a vice, and sharpened by drawing the polished back of a gouge along the edges, at an angle of about 60°. A proper scraper sharpener is a piece of $\frac{1}{8}$ in. or $\frac{1}{4}$ in. round polished steel fixed in an ordinary tool handle. When the scrapers become dull, draw the gouge or

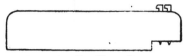

Fig. 42.—Purfling Gauge.

sharpener flat along the sides ; this turns the " burr " to the edge again ; then sharpen them in the vice as at first.

Several half-round files, different sizes, and of varying degrees of fineness, will be necessary.

Purfling tools include a special form of cutting gauge, a knife, and a picker or router.

The simplest form of purfling gauge can be made as follows :—Take a scrap of hard wood, about 4 in. by 1 in. by $\frac{3}{4}$ in., and cut a cheek about 1 in. long and $\frac{1}{2}$ in. deep at one end. At exactly $\frac{5}{32}$ in. from this cheek drive in a small steel brad, and file it to a sharp point with a fine file. This, of course, makes but one cut at a time.

A better but still very simple gauge is shown in Fig. 42. The wooden part is shaped as before; then insert two steel brads about $\frac{1}{16}$ in. apart, and file to a nice cutting edge both ways. Try the gauge on a waste scrap of pine to see that the cuts are just the width of the purfling apart.

A still better purfling gauge is shown by Figs. 43 and
44 To make it, take a piece of hard wood about 4 in.
long, 1½ in. broad, and ¾ in. thick, and shape it as Figs.
43 and 44. The cutter A may be made from a piece of
steel about 2 in. long cut from a joiner's nail-punch.
File the steel parallel, and with a thin ward file cut a
groove about ⅛ in. deep in one end, forming a double
cutter as Fig 45, taking care that the over-all size is just
the width of the purfling. A side view of the end is

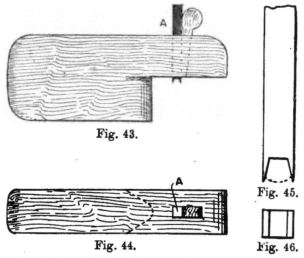

Fig. 43.

Fig. 44.

Fig. 45.

Fig. 46.

Figs. 43 and 44.—Purfling Gauge. Figs. 45 and 46.—Cutter
of Purfling Gauge.

circular as shown by dotted lines. Fig. 46 is a plan of
the cutter looking upwards. The cutter should be filed
up sharp with a fine file, but will cut cleaner and keep
its edge longer if tempered and set up with a thin slip of
oilstone. After the double cut (which must be done
with a firm hand) is made all round the violin tables, the
groove is cleaned out with a narrow chisel or a sharp
bradawl.

Another useful form of purfling gauge, easily made
and very effective, is illustrated by Fig. 47. A is a

sliding bar carrying the cutter and wedge, B is the
wedge for fixing the sliding bar, and C is a hardwood
stock with the bottom rounded on one side as at D.
The method of using is to set the cutter, which must be
well sharpened, to the required distance, and to go round

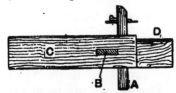

Fig. 47.—Another Purfling Gauge.

the instrument, being very careful not to cut too deep ;
then reduce the width by $\frac{1}{16}$ in. and cut the outer line.
The wood between the lines can then be picked out with
a bent purfling chisel, and the purfling fitted and glued.

The purfling knife (Fig. 48) is an erasing knife
ground to a long keen point. Two or three of these
knives should be at hand ; they are used for deepening
the groove in which to lay the purfling, for truing the
mitred corners of the purfling, for trimming the sound
holes, and many minor purposes, and should be kept as
sharp as a razor.

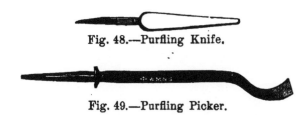

Fig. 48.—Purfling Knife.

Fig. 49.—Purfling Picker.

The purfling picker or router is a bent chisel, of which
Fig. 49 gives an idea, used for removing the material
between the two lines cut with the purfling gauge.
Sometimes a sharp bradawl can be used for this purpose.

CHAPTER II.

MAKING VIOLIN MOULDS.

VIOLIN moulds are of two kinds—the inside mould and the outside mould—and it is the former kind which can alone be obtained in England. Fig. 50 shows an outside and Fig. 51 an inside mould. A violin is

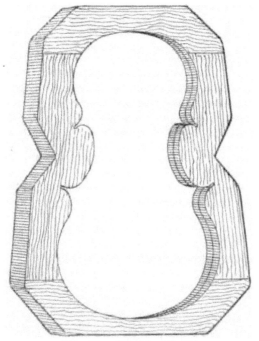

Fig. 50.—Outside Mould.

built outside an inside mould, or inside an outside mould. It is of the very first importance that a mould should be true and the wood perfectly seasoned.

Outside moulds are far easier to make and far cheaper,

and the best of those in use by manufacturers are made
of iron. For making an outside mould in wood,
beech is best, but it is very slow wood to season, even if
stoved, and the mould in its weakest parts is very liable
to split. Obtain a true 3-ft. length, 11 in. wide and 1 in.
thick, of plain maple. Cut this into two lengths of
18 in. ; they will be found not "true." Therefore, place
them against each other, the hollows face to face, and
clamp them together with three screws along the middle of

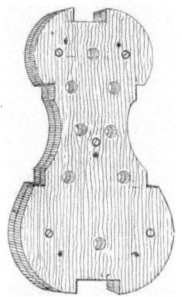

Fig. 51.—Inside Mould.

the length, with one screw in the middle and the others
about 5 in. above and below, so that the screw holes will
come away when the centre of the mould is cut out.
Place these screwed-up boards in a moderately heated
oven daily for a week, and after that no more shrinkage
will occur. Then unscrew the boards and most carefully
true each face, so as not to have the boards "in
winding."

There are practically four kinds of moulds—Stradi-

varius, Guarnerius, Amati, and Stainer, and it is
impossible to alter these patterns without spoiling the
whole fiddle.

To copy a fiddle the worker is usually directed to
place it on its back over a piece of white paper, and trace
the outline ; but this does not give the true outline,
because of the bulging of the back. Therefore, if
possible, remove the back of the violin and place it, inside
down, on the paper. If not, avoid outlines which can be
bought and which are too often traced from an unopened
fiddle, which give very different results from those
obtained from a separate back. Avoid the small Amati
pattern ; choose rather either the Guarnerian or Stradi-
varian forms, these being larger ; it is then still possible
to use the pretty Amati arching and thickness, when the
charming but feeble Amati tone will be strengthened by
the larger outlines of the other two shapes.

Do not take a complete outline. The best way of
copying a violin is to take half an outline, turn it over,
and add the rest from the same tracing. In finishing,
the fiddle edges will be a trifle out, but the error will be
much less than if a whole outline is treated at the start.
Therefore, trace with a very finely pointed H pencil a
half outline on a piece of tough official paper. This is
better than tracing on to a thin plank, as sometimes
advised, because it needs no squaring with chisel and file.
The paper should be at least 14 in. by 9 in. for the half
outline of the model, a line down the middle of the length
of the paper having first been drawn with a straightedge.
Then turn the half outline over very carefully, and trace
it again so as to obtain the shape of the violin. Four
fine pins may be used to prevent slipping, and note that
the paper must not double up at all. Next, with a
pair of fine scissors cut inside the pencil mark very
exactly ; this is necessary, or the extra thickness of even
the pencil line will spoil the fine outline.

Now screw the two prepared boards together again.
Draw a pencil line down the middle of the length, and
at 2 in. from one end place the wide end of the outline

so that the centre line of the paper outline corresponds
exactly with the line on the wood. Fix with pins, and
draw the outline on the wood. It will then be possible
to see where to bore screw holes so as not to weaken
the mould or interfere with the outline, and at the
same time firmly secure the two boards together so
as to form one. The best situations are indicated in
Fig. 52. Countersink the holes ¼ in., but 1 in. screws
will be the extreme length, and shorter screws will be
better if the countersink is increased. The hole in the
upper board should be larger than that in the lower so
as to draw the two boards closely together, the screws
being, of, course, greased. Once more face truly the
board with the countersunk holes, thus obliterating the
pattern, which was only drawn to secure safe positions
for the screws. Now square and true all the edges,
which in the case of the ends is most important. Square
from the now true pattern face, and turn over to the
back and plane down until one end is a trifle more than
1¼ in. thick, and the other end exactly 1⅜ in., each
surface and edge being smooth. This will give the
mould 1¼ in. depth at the lower end, and 1⅜ in. at the
upper by final sandpapering.

There is now the difficult task of drawing two
patterns exactly opposite each other on a thick piece of
wood. If they are not exactly opposite, the ribs will
bulge or be hollow. Remember the wood is a wedge,
not a solid parallelogram, and squaring must be done
from the countersunk face, and not from the slanting
face. Now draw a fine pencil line truly down the
middle of the countersunk face, which will be the back
or under surface of the mould, and before removing the
straight-edge, firmly draw a sharply pointed marking
awl down the line. Place the paper pattern with its
centre line exactly over the line on the wood, its lower
and wider end being 2 in. from the thick (1¼ in.) end of
the wedge. Secure the pattern with pins driven in
upright, and make a fine tracing of the violin pattern on
the wood, taking care that the side with the F holes is

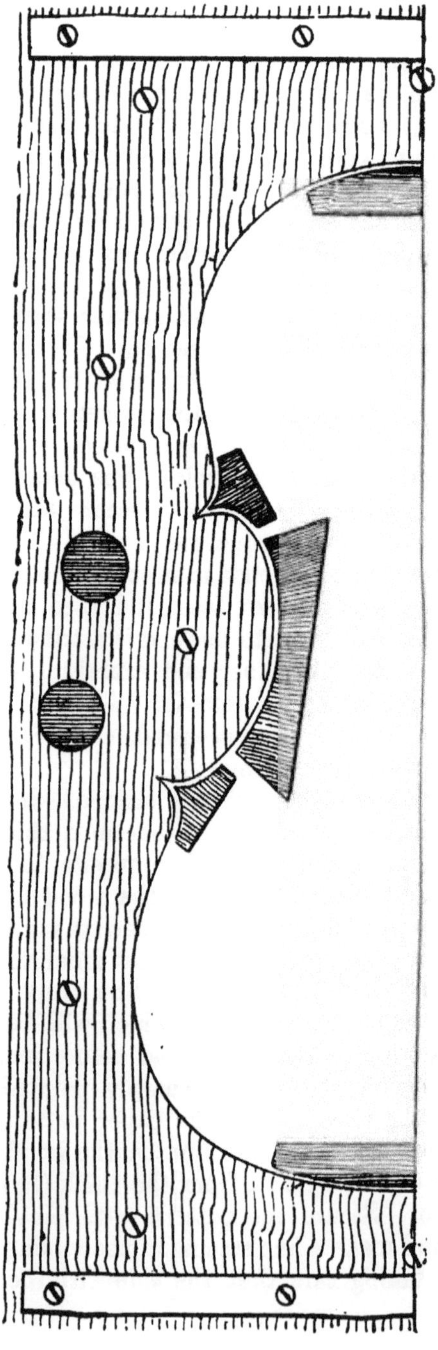

Fig. 52.—Half of Outside Mould.

undermost. This precaution is necessary so as to lose the error of even the thickness of the paper. Before removing the paper run a finger along its edges to steady them, and delicately, so as not to push aside the paper in the least, make a mark with the awl exactly in the pencil mark. Then go over the mark again so as to deepen it, the first serving as a channel guide, and it is well to sharpen the pencil again and re-pencil the last awl mark. Add the "button" at the thin upper end, and if mistakes have been avoided so far, a great part of the difficulty is over. Now bore the large bit holes outside the figure. These must be upright, and are for the ends of the iron clamps which tighten the corner blocks of the violin.

The delicate task of drawing an inner outline $\frac{3}{4}$ in. from the one just drawn is now to be undertaken. It must be exact, as the figure it describes has to be cut out. A skilled worker may trust to his eye, but finely pointed compasses will be found useful. So far no pattern has been drawn on the front face of the mould. Draw a square line over the two edges, and thence along the middle of the new face to be exactly opposite the first line drawn on the wood at the start. No pains must be spared to get these middle lines truly opposite, the two faces being tested by "opposite" squaring. Deeply mark this new line. Now make two points in it at the same distance from the edges as the extremities of the fiddle outline are from their edges. Then proceed to draw the second outline. But it is not necessary to trust solely to the end squares to get these points. Bore at each end two large centre-bit holes fairly close to the inner line (on no account infringe on it or bore untruly), and by flat gouges and chisels square also from inside; then if the squaring is true at each end, and also at the upper and lower ends of the inside, the work is correct. Now carefully fix the paper pattern on the new surface, the side of the paper with the F holes being uppermost, and trace and mark exactly as before, also drawing the inner line (no awl mark being needed in the inner pattern), but do not add the button to the figure.

The joiner will now easily cut away the wood inside the inner outline, but the amateur may bore with a large bit numerous holes all round the inside, not working nearer than $\frac{1}{16}$ in. from the inner line. The bit holes should not run into each other, and the bit needs greasing. Now with a mallet and chisel cut away the inside wood. With flat carving gouges and chisels work up to the inner pencil line, squaring incessantly when nearing it, but always from the belly face, when scrapers will be necessary. Before working out the corners, saw the lines in the figure with a fine dovetail saw. Do the work mainly with a penknife on the front and back, and deepen the upper and lower (back and belly), knife corner cuts till at last the cut is complete; then with fine chisels finish the corners.

The saw line is prolonged to have extra space when fitting the ribs; $\frac{1}{8}$ in. beyond the ends of the corners of the violin outline is ample; more would weaken the mould. Now with a chisel deepen the tips of the corners and make parallel cuts exactly where the inner corners end. The latter helps in marking where the ribs are to be trimmed off when out of the mould. It is useful also to join the two centre lines at the ends, inside the mould. Also as the lines, especially the corners and middle lines, become worn out, renew them with pencil and awl.

The outside mould is now complete. The difficult cramping blocks of the inside mould are dispensed with, which is an advantage, because if the blocks are not made very truly, they are troublesome, the work of fitting the hollows in the inside mould being far more difficult than anything in the outside mould just described. Again, the difficulty of affixing the linings in the inside mould is very great, as it is impossible to see whether the under edges gape or not, and bad-fitting joints are very liable to occur.

Cramping blocks are supposed to be made with

outside moulds, but for the mould just described, false corner blocks and little sticks can be used.

The mould should be tested from time to time. To do this, fasten with four screws in each, two steel bars 1 in. wide and ¼ in. deep at each end, on, say, the back surface. Any deviation can then be noticed by applying a piece of cardboard either under the middle or the ends of the bars. Two boards are used instead of one, because of the difficulty, away from a town, of getting seasoned wood of the proper thickness. Also by unscrewing and removing one piece, the side linings can be clipped very conveniently. This mould should not be kept in a very warm place nor in the sunlight, and it is well, when taking up violin making as a hobby, to have several moulds, it being usual to have a dozen sets, say, of violin bodies in hand at once. Then back, belly, and neck can be added, finished off, and left to season, it being useless to varnish till the summer. ⟨When the inside edges of the mould bulge a little where they ought not to, it is of little consequence, if anywhere between the corners and end blocks, providing the bulging (or hollowing), is repeated the whole depth so as to square well, as the rib will not follow small errors, but sweeps past them. The corners are the vital parts of a mould. The ends also must be flat, not askew, or they should be only just slightly rounded off.

The above method of mould making is recommended; but one other way is of advantage because it produces two moulds at one operation—one outside and one inside. Obtain a piece of well-seasoned straight hardwood, as beech, birch, or sycamore, 17 in. long by 9½ in. broad at one end, tapering to 8½ in. at the other, and 1¾ in. thick. Plane this piece perfectly true in length and breadth, and finish it 1⁵⁄₁₆ in. thick at the broad end, tapering to 1¼ in. at the narrow end. Now make a line down the middle from end to end with a sharp awl, and afterwards trace the line with lead pencil to make it more legible. Instructions given in the next chapter on violin making will refer to the patterns represented by

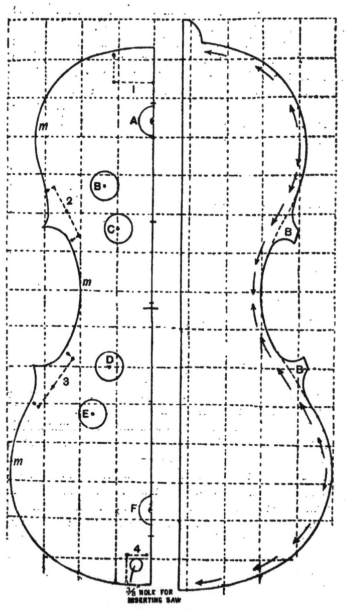

⅜ HOLE FOR
INSERTING SAW

Fig. 54.—Inside Pattern.   Fig. 53.—Outside Pattern

Figs. 53 and 54 ; therefore cut out these patterns in zinc or thin wood, taking care to have all the marks on Fig. 54 quite distinct. Fig. 53 shows the outside pattern, and Fig. 54 the inside pattern. Place the inside pattern exactly to the centre line on the block, and an equal distance from each end, and carefully, but decidedly, trace round the pattern with the marker

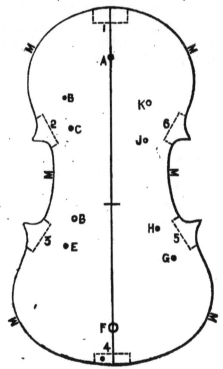

Fig. 55.—Mould Block ready for Sawing Out.

following with lead pencil. Then mark through the pattern the position of each block, as shown by the dotted lines in Fig. 54, and also the centres for the holes, A to F. Now turn the pattern over, and mark the other side in precisely the same manner ; on the accuracy of this operation the ultimate balance of the fiddle depends. When ready to be sawn out, the block should bear every

one of the marks which appear in Fig. 55. With a ⅜ in.
bit bore the hole for inserting the saw. The models can
now be cut out with a bow saw, or, preferably, with a
fret or jigger saw, making a cut of $\frac{1}{12}$th of an inch, and
going exactly round the line, M, M, M, subsequently
cutting out the recesses, 1, 2, 3, 4, 5, 6.

The edges of both models should now be trimmed up,
by placing each of the models edgewise in a wooden
vice, and, with a file, one end held in each hand, taking
out all the small ridges which the saw has made, still
keeping both models square to the side on which the
outline was traced. Write distinctly on both models the
word "back," so as to avoid confusion. Next, with a
¾-in. bit bore the holes, A to K. Square the centre line
down each of the end block recesses 1 and 4, and with a
straightedge make another centre line the entire length
of the other side of model. There are now two well-
finished models, inside and outside.

There is a method of building violins without using
a mould. First, the back is prepared, and then the
blocks are glued directly upon it in their proper places.
The ribs are bent to fit nicely, and with their linings are
then glued in position. Finally, the belly is glued on.
This may not appear easy, but a skilful worker saves a
lot of time and trouble in this way, and the model can
be altered at will during the process.

41

CHAPTER III.

VIOLIN MAKING.

WORK on a Stradivarius model (see Figs. 1, 53, and 54) can be begun by jointing the back and the belly, the pieces for which should be cut through as in Fig. 3 (p. 11). The insides of each piece should be planed quite true. Always plane the back across the grain, otherwise the plane will jerk pieces out of it. Placing the true side downwards on the shooting board, with the trying plane make along the thick edge a perfectly square joint. This, to an unpractised hand, will be a matter of great difficulty, and should a bad joint be made it may not be possible to remedy it without making the wood too small. When both pieces are planed so true that the light cannot be seen between them, hold both edges before the fire till quite warm, and then fasten one piece in the bench vice with the planed side towards the worker. Place the other piece with the true edge touching it, and very quickly go over both edges with fresh, hot glue. Now put the loose piece in position, and rub it slowly backwards and forwards, pressing firmly the while. When as much glue as possible has been pressed out, which will be known by the amount of suction that ensues, and the pieces are quite even sponge the joint both sides with hot water and remove the jointed piece from the vice. Put it aside to set, and proceed to joint the other pieces. Whilst the back and belly are laid away to harden, take the inside model (Fig. 54, p. 38) and into each of the six recesses glue a piece of the 1-in. pine, width to suit, and rather longer than the depth of model; use only a small quantity of glue for the back of each block, as the pieces will have to be forced out again when the ribs are finished; but for safety cramp them into position with iron cramps, and put the whole in a warm place to dry. After the joints are thoroughly hard (twelve hours at least should be allowed), plane the flat sides of each piece quite true every way—lengthwise, crosswise, and diagonally.

For "truing up" the back, a violin maker advises the use of a plane of the same size as a "jack" plane, but having a coarse-toothed iron, almost vertical. For truing the belly use the trying plane.

The back and belly are now ready for marking from the ribs, and as the ribs are not made they must be got together. Take the inside model into which the six blocks have been glued, and plane these down to the level of the model, but take care not to injure the latter in doing so. With a straight-edge continue the centre lines on the model across each of the end blocks. Place the inside pattern to the centre line and even with the model all round, and then carefully trace the outline on the blocks ; now turn the pattern and mark the other blocks in the same way. This done, write on each block, inside the marks, figures corresponding with those on the model, and repeat the whole process on the other side. With a No. 4 gouge (see Fig. 22, p. 17) cut out the hollows in the insides of the waist blocks ; if the wood is cutting inwards turn the model over and cut from the other side. Do not cut within the marks, and carve only the insides of the waist blocks at present. Make twenty light cuts rather than one too deep. Fix the model edgewise in a wooden vice, and, with the round side of a file to fit the sweep, take out all the inequalities which may have been made in carving, and make the hollows square across. The filing gives a better gluing surface for attaching the ribs.

The next operation is to prepare the rib strips for bending. With one of the iron cramps fasten one of the strips by its extreme end to the bench, inserting a small piece of wood or cork under the cramp so as not to damage the rib; and with the veneer plane work from the clamp to the end of rib, and take off the rough part of the wood. Now loose the cramp, turn the rib end for end, and plane the part previously hidden by the cramp. When all the strips have been treated in the same way, fix them on the bench again, and with a flat scraper which must be very sharp, take out all the plane marks. Use the scraper diagonally, to cross the figure of the wood. Divide the strips with a sharp knife, and the square into lengths of 5½, 7½, and 9½ in. One strip will make two top or 7½ in. ribs and the two others will each make one bottom and one waist rib.

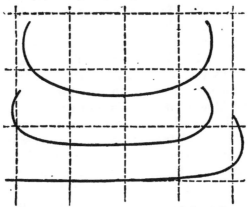

Fig. 56.—Stages in Bending Waist Ribs.

The bending of the ribs demands steadiness, care, and patience, as accidents are very likely to happen, and another rib may have to be planed up. Assuming that the bending apparatus (shown by Fig. 5, p. 12) is used, fix it in an iron vice, attach an indiarubber tube from the gas to the heater, and light the gas, but observe that it does not light at the wrong place. Turn the gas very low, and when the tube is sufficiently hot to scorch very slightly a piece of paper held on it, the ribs may be bent as shown in Fig. 56. Begin with the waist ribs, and make sure that the figure of all the ribs matches in inclination; it is better to mark each rib to the blocks before bending any of them. Do not hurry the bending, and use only gentle pressure. When hot enough, the ribs may be bent any way desired.   Have at hand a small bucket containing cold water and a sponge, and if the tube gets too hot, cool it slightly with water.   Frequently try the waist ribs in course of bending into the places already prepared for their reception.   The others may be bent to fit the inside pattern.

For a first attempt at bending, wood with rather a plain figure should be chosen, this being easier to bend and work.   The proper heat is just short of scorching the wood, and may be tested by trial on spare pieces. If too much heat is used, there is a danger of making the ribs brittle.   By moving the rib backwards and forwards over the hot tube it will soon become pliable. If the apparatus shown by Figs. 6 and 7 is used, the top edge of the tube will form the quick bends, whilst the sides can be used for the flatter parts.   When the proper bend is obtained, put the rib into the mould and leave it until cold, when it will retain its shape.

A caul or small block can now be cut from the 1 in. pine to fit each of the hollows.   Mark the cauls to their places, and put them on a stove or near the fire to get hot ; this causes the glue to set much sooner.   Coat one of the waist blocks with glue, place the hot caul against it, and putting the end of an iron cramp into the hole exactly facing the hollow, cramp it close up, but see that both edges are a little " proud " of the model.   It is not possible to glue both ends of each rib at one operation ; let one end set before gluing the other, as the cramps might be in the way of each other.   When all the ends of waist ribs are fast, in proper positions, cut the ribs down level with the model by means of a flat toothing plane.

Now carve the remaining blocks in the same way as the waists, but cut through the end of each waist rib as well as the block to which it is attached, otherwise a bad joint may result.   Correctly file all the six blocks, make cauls to fit each, and mark them to their places. Glue and fix each of the corners, leaving the top and bottom until the last.   There is no necessity to make a joint with the ribs at the top, as both ends will be cut away when the neck is fixed. If the bottom joint of ribs is not good, the defect may be remedied by inserting a piece of purfling or fancy wood, but this must be exactly true to the centre mark. A narrow strip of ebony can be inserted; this looks very well [when finished, the bottom nut or rest crossing the top of this piece making the letter T.

When the ribs are firmly set, plane them down to the model, and finish them in the following way: set the compasses to 3¾ in., and from the point where the short line crosses the centre line of model, describe a circle, whose circumference gives the points at which the ribs should be square across. Fasten the model edgewise in the vice, and file each curve square across and free from inequalities, and make the entire set of ribs an equal thickness. After this has been nicely done, scrape them over, and rub down with three or four grades of glasspaper, the last one very fine. Use the glasspaper wrapped round a cork rubber, and work lengthwise of the ribs, preserving the edges quite square and sharp. Now square a light centre line down the bottom of the ribs, and midway of this centre line make a puncture which will show the position of the end pin, the hole for which should then be bored with a ¼-in. bit.

The ribs are now ready, and the back and belly can be marked out from them; but first place the outside pattern (Fig. 53, p. 38) to the joint of the back, and trace round it with lead pencil; turn the pattern over, and complete the outline. Next place the mould, back downwards, exactly true to the centre joint, and an equal distance all round from the pencil outline already traced, and fasten it in that position with an iron cramp at each end. Now correctly trace on the back the outline of the ribs with a fine pointed marker, and then remove the model, and mark out the belly in the the same way as the back; but as the "tab" or "button" on the latter will not be required on the belly, the outline must therefore be continued across the top.

Sawing out the back and belly with the bow or fret-saw, keeping just outside the pencil mark, is the next business. With the compasses make a line all round the upper or bevelled sides of both back and belly, ⅜ in. from the edge. Now set the cutting gauge to $\frac{3}{16}$ in. and cut an incisive line that distance from the flat side, all round both back and belly. With a dovetail saw or fine tenon saw, and gouges, cut away the rectangular piece thus described, and afterwards level it with a flat oval thumb-plane and files, finishing it to a thickness of $\frac{5}{32}$ in. The mould, with the ribs on, should again be placed in the position marked from them on the back, cramped as before, and fixed in the vice, thus fastening securely the back and the ribs together. The edges should now be reduced with files until there is a perfectly even projection over the ribs of ⅛ in. Carefully make the corners match in direction as shown in Fig. 57. Remove the mould from the vice, and take the cramps off; now open the compasses to $\frac{7}{16}$ in., place one point on the joint of the tab ⅛ in. from the rib line, and describe a semicircle; this gives the form the tab will bear, or nearly so.

Fig. 58 shows a view of the back with edge reduced ready for purfling, a process that will now be described. Two carving blocks are now required. Get two pieces of deal 15 in. by 9 in. by 1 in. or 1¼ in., plane one side of each piece true, and mark the outline of the ribs on each planed side, and have the shapes cut out with a band saw. In both of the rough sides bore a small hole central of length and width, and tap a thread in it with the point of the carver's screw, using the wing nut as a wrench. The back and belly should each be glued on one of these carving-blocks, by putting a dab of glue about 3 in. from each end, and cramping them to the blocks with iron cramps or with hand-screws. In a few hours these will be set, and the rough modelling and purfling can be proceeded with.

For the modelling, turn the carving screw firmly into the block on which the back is glued, put the screw

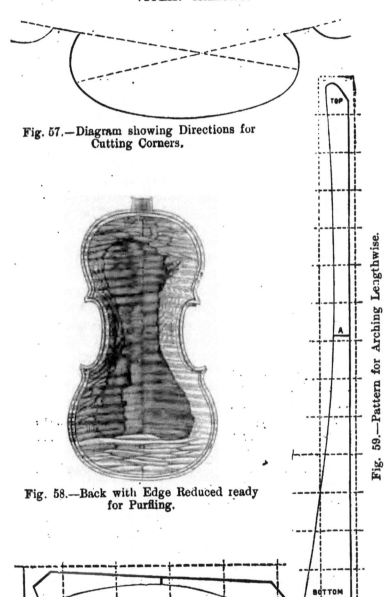

Fig. 57.—Diagram showing Directions for Cutting Corners.

Fig. 58.—Back with Edge Reduced ready for Purfling.

Fig. 59.—Pattern for Arching Lengthwise.

Fig. 60.—Pattern for Arching Across Waist.

through the bench, and turn the nut up to the under side, of the bench.   It is better to work the back first, as it will be first required.   Now with a smoothing plane, across the grain, give the arching, roughly, of Fig. 59 (Fig. 60 is the pattern for the arching across the waist at A).   Afterwards with a No. 4 gouge (see Fig. 22, p. 17) take off the thick parts of the wood, and aim to give a curve from the $\frac{3}{8}$ in. line to the centre joint.

The purfling tool must now be set with one blade $\frac{5}{32}$ in. from the stock or shoulder, and the other exactly $\frac{1}{16}$ in. further away.   A double line must now be traced all round, distinct, but not too deep ; the lines must then be cut deeper with a fine, keen-pointed knife (Fig. 48, p. 29), always cutting off the end of the grain.   The grooves should be cut to a depth of $\frac{1}{12}$th of an inch, which is the depth the purfling should be.

The piece of wood between the lines in the waists only should now be taken out with the router or bent chisel, the greatest care being taken not to go through or split any pieces from the edge of the groove.   The dark line in Fig. 61 is intended to represent the way in which the groove should be cut when ready to receive the purfling. A piece of purfling should be cut to fill this groove completely ; when fitted, run glue all through the groove, and tap the purfling into its place with a small hammer. With a sponge dipped in hot water remove the glue, and rub the purfling more perfectly down with the tail end of the hammer.   When both waists are purfled, lay the back aside to dry, and proceed in like manner with the belly.   It will be remembered that the "tab" prevented the gauge from going completely round the back. The lines must therefore be joined with the compasses, care being taken to preserve the sweep or curve.

The whole of the grooves will now be ready for cutting, and the utmost care will be necessary in making the mitres at each corner, as also the joints in the pieces of purfling.   The purfling already in the waists will require to be cut down in the direction shown by line a a (Fig. 61).   The next business is to

make the mitres on the pieces of purfling, which must
be done so well that the points of both inner and outer
blacks as well as the whites finish together at a very
acute angle. It is said that in the Cremonese purfling
the outer black is run a little beyond the meeting point ;
the delicacy of this apparently trifling process will be
best appreciated by those who try to do it. After all
the mitres are fitted to their places, make bevels at the
other end of each piece in such a manner that when
glued in the joint will not be perceptible. It may be
found more convenient to put the upper and lower
rounds of purfling in, each in two pieces, as the mitres
can be made much safer and better than when only one

Fig. 61.—Diagram Showing Method of Purfling Waists
and Cutting Mitres.

length is used. When purfling the belly, do not
attempt to make joints at either top or bottom ; the
insertion of the neck in one case, and of the bottom nut
in the other, will obviate all necessity for doing so.
When all the purfling is laid and rubbed down, sponge
the edges all over with hot water ; this will not only
take off all glue from the surface, but will make the
purfling fit better. Now put aside to dry while purfling
the belly, which being accomplished, take the back in
hand again. Open the compasses to $\frac{3}{16}$th of an inch,
and trace a line round the back that distance from the
edge. Fix the screw through the bench as before, and
following the direction of the arrows in Fig. 53 (p. 38)
with a No. 6 gouge (see Fig. 22, p. 17), cut a hollow
D

between the compass line and outer edge of purfling all
round, leaving the corners, B, B, until last. If by mis-
chance the edge of the hollow is made irregular, go
round again with the gouge, this time a little over the
purfling, and cut in opposite direction to the arrows.
When the hollow is satisfactorily carved, complete the
lengthways arching (Fig. 59) with a flat gouge and oval
thumb-plane.   Then give (at A, Fig. 59) the requisite
form across the waist with a No. 4 gouge ; after having
done this, with a No. 2 gouge and small planes gradually "melt" the archings into the hollow all round,
taking care that the hollow be not damaged ; if the
wood cuts rough, reverse the cutting.   Do not attempt
to carve the wrong way of the wood.

With the scrapers, very sharp, take out all plane
marks, and with No. 1½ glasspaper used on cork rubbers,
gently rub down all over, but do not spoil the modelling
in doing this.   Brush off all the dust, and sponge all
over with cold water ; and whilst the back is drying,
model the belly in the way described.   By the time this
is finished the back will be ready for another scraping
and glasspapering—this time with finer paper.   Should
any inequalities be shown up by the wetting, these
must be removed with the scrapers before papering.
After this operation is performed, again sponge the
work over.   The belly should now be attended to in
the same way.

To bend purfling round sharp corners, dip the end
into boiling water for an instant, but not long enough
to loosen the glue which holds the strips together.

There is no good substitute for purfling.   Some of the
old makers used to paint lines round the margin to
imitate purfling, but this plan is now adopted only in
very inferior instruments.

The next business will be the manipulation of the
ribs and their attachment to back and belly.   The ribs
should now be taken off the mould by inserting a knife
between each block and the mould, and giving the knife
a tap with the hammer.   In this way break the glue

which holds the blocks and the mould together. When all are loose, gradually press the blocks out of the mould, but be careful not to loose any of the ribs in doing so. The ribs should at once be placed in the outside mould or frame, and have the linings put in them. (Fig. 62 shows the ribs with the linings in, the blocks being carved and finished). Take the lining strips and file one edge to a nice round or bevel, whichever is fancied, and cut them to fit in between the blocks; make each end which touches either top or bottom blocks a little wedge

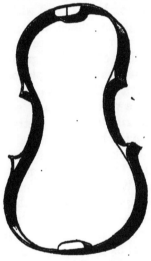

Fig. 62.—Set of Ribs with Linings.

shaped, so that when glued and pressed into position they will fit tight; leave them a little "proud" of the ribs.

When all the eight upper and lower bout linings are in place, sponge all glue off, and attend to the waists. Of course, the linings of these will require to be bent in the opposite direction to those already put in, and may be run into or only just made to fit between the blocks 2 and 3, 5 and 6 (Fig. 55, p. 39). If the latter method is adopted the ribs should, when all linings are fitted, be drawn ¼ in. out of the mould, and the linings fastened at each end until set with a cramp (Fig. 14, p. 15). When these are set, press the ribs through the other side of the mould, and fix the two other linings. Another way to fix linings is to make blocks to fit all over the linings of each waist, and cramp them to the mould. Still another way, is to cut a groove in each block with a $\frac{1}{16}$ in. chisel, and run the linings into these grooves. When dry, plane the linings level with the ribs, reduce the top block to $\frac{3}{4}$ in., the bottom one to $\frac{4}{4}$ in., and round the corners off with a No. 3 or No. 4 gouge. Next, with a flat gouge carve the remaining blocks level with the linings, giving the inside the guitar shape, and glasspaper all round the insides, using a rubber, to prevent the sharp corners of the gluing edge of the linings being taken off. A great deal of taste may be displayed in lining and in carving the blocks. The linings may be put in and the blocks carved in a variety of ways, some of which make the inside of the ribs look very pretty.

Having given the back a final glasspapering, take it off the carving-block by forcing a knife between the two from each end. The back can now be marked from inside the ribs. With fiddle cramps fasten the ribs into the position originally traced from the outsides, and mark round the insides with thick leadpencil; now remove the ribs and replace them in the frame. This done, cut two pieces of deal 5½ in. long by 1 in. by 1¼ in., and glue on them the three pieces of wood, ¼ in. thick, shown at A (Fig. 63). Instead of gluing these pieces on, the blocks may be recessed ⅛ in. if desired, but the first way is simpler. As soon as the hollowing blocks are ready, lay them on the bench, put the back upon them in the position obviously aid out for it, and through a hole in the bench at each end pass one of the iron cramps, and with a protecting piece of wood, about 2 in. long, on the back, and under each cramp, screw the latter up tight. Next put pieces of cork 3 in. long, 1 in. wide, and depth to fit under and across each corner; also a small piece under the joint midway of its length. Do not put these pieces in too

tight, but just sufficient to make the back solid. With
a No. 4 gouge carefully proceed to hollow, working very
steadily, and cutting from inside the pencil mark to the
joint. Take only small cuts, constantly trying the thicknesses with the thicknessing gauge until half the back is
hollowed to $\frac{1}{32}$ in. more than the dimensions indicated
given in Fig. 64. (In this figure and in Fig. 65 the
numbers refer to thirty-seconds of an inch). The $\frac{1}{32}$ in. is
to allow for toothing, scraping and papering. One side
being roughly hollowed, turn the back round, and work

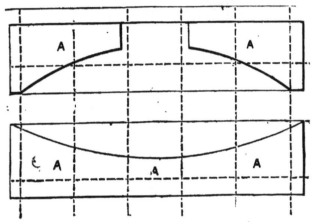

Fig. 63.—Blocks for Hollowing.

the other half in the same way. The thicknesses given
in Figs. 64 and 65 are not, of course, absolute; the
varying qualities of wood will necessitate slight modifications. The gouging being finished, with a tooth plane
reduce to a shade above the proper thickness, and then
finish with the scrapers. Do not be afraid of using the
gauge too frequently. (In Chapter I. is described a
special appliance for thicknessing backs and bellies, and
its use will save a lot of the labour indicated above.)

After scraping and finally adjusting the thickness,
glasspaper all the inside to a good face. The edges may
now be rounded with the round side of a rather fine
file, taking off the square edges, and making the entire

projection from purfling to rib-line a beautiful roll.
Then paper up without destroying the roundness of the
edge, wrap it up, and put it out of the way. Do not
attempt to do anything with the tab yet.

The belly, still on the carving-block, will now require
fine glasspapering, and the sound-holes to be marked on

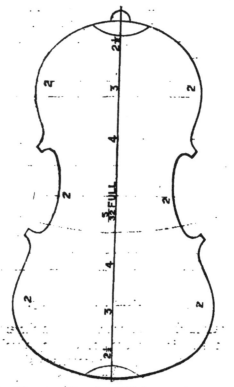

Fig. 64.—Diagram Showing Thickness of Violin Back.

it. Place the pattern (Fig. 66) parallel with the joint
(which will, if all has been carried out as described, be
exactly central), with its centre mark, A, 6½ in. from the
bottom of centre joint. Then with a very fine pencil,
and with the greatest care, trace inside the pattern.
Now reverse the pattern in exactly the corresponding
position, and mark in the same manner. The circular

holes must now be cut out with punches or centre-bits. With punches the position is easily determined ; press the punch, and at the same time give a circular motion to it, thus cutting a clean hole—if right through, so much the better. If a centre-bit is used, take care that it is absolutely central, and do not lay on too hard, or points B, B, will be shaken and afterwards broken off.

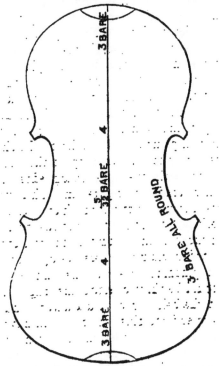

Fig. 65.—Diagram Showing Thickness of Violin Belly.

Now follow the pencil line with a knife, cutting in the direction of the arrows. The straight lines, C, C, must be cut from the points. Sound-holes may also be cut out with a fret saw.

The belly should now be taken off the carving-block and hollowed in the way described for the back, or nearly so, as, being different wood, it will require a

little different treatment. When the hollowing, scraping, and papering are finished, trim the sound-holes
with the knife and small files, and cut the V's.

The bass-bar, the usual shape of which is shown by
Fig. 67, should next be fitted as follows: First plane it
down to $\frac{3}{16}$ in., and cut it square off at $10\frac{1}{2}$ in. Make
a pencil line nearly parallel with the joint, but $\frac{3}{16}$ in.
distant from it, down the right-hand side, and $1\frac{3}{4}$ in.
from both top and bottom outside edges; make $\frac{1}{4}$ in.
marks at right angles with the pencil mark. The
position of the bar is now fully marked out. With the
flat gouge roughly fit the bar to its place, keeping it
perfectly upright. Chalk the bar position well over
with a piece of billiard-chalk, and putting the bar close
outside the pencil mark, draw it slightly backwards and
forwards, pressing gently downwards all the time.
With a flat oval plane carefully take off the chalk marks
which appear on the bar, and repeat the process until
the chalk shows all over the fitting edge of the bar,
when it will be ready to be glued in. This may take a
few minutes or it may take a long while, but it must be
done properly. Now remove all the chalk with a dust-
brush, glue the bar, and cramp it in position with the
bass-bar wooden cramps—these cramps are U-shaped
and have a pinching screw at the end. A little fine
sawdust should be thrown along the angles formed by
the bar and the belly, then with a narrow chisel remove
both sawdust and the glue which it will have taken up.
When the bar is quite set, plane it down to the right
size $\frac{5}{8}$ in. deep at the point where a line between the two
inner V's of the sound-holes would cross it, and gradually diminish with a slight curve to $\frac{1}{16}$ in. at each end.
The bass-bar should be placed exactly under the left
foot of the bridge, not quite parallel with the centre
line of the belly, but inclining nearer the centre at the
neck, and further away at the tail-piece end. It should
be placed equi-distant from each end. The accepted
method of glueing in a bass-bar "with a spring" is
described on p. 76.

With coarse glasspaper, followed by fine, the top should next be made round. The edges of the belly should now be made round in the manner described for the back. The sound-holes, when finished, will be rather larger than the pattern, as they have been traced inside a zinc pattern, and it is intended that all the lines should be cut away.

Before fixing the ribs to the back, the blocks should

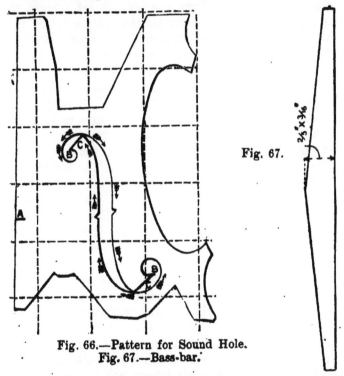

Fig. 67.

Fig. 66.—Pattern for Sound Hole.
Fig. 67.—Bass-bar.

be sized by giving them a good coat of glue, then burning the glue with a hot iron, afterwards rasping off the burnt glue. This effectually stops the blocks from absorbing any more glue. A coat of very thin glue on the rib edges is also beneficial. The ribs may now be glued ; place them on the back to the position marked from the outsides, and cramp down the end blocks with iron cramps, having a piece of wood between cramp and

back, to prevent the latter being marked, and also to
extend the pressure over the blocks. Use the violin
cramps all round, and when all are secure, sponge all the
glue from inside.

: After a few hours, clean the inside with fine glass-
paper, affix a label, and glue the belly on. If any glue
should run down the inside, sponge it out directly, as
there will not be another chance; but be quick, or the
glue will be cold. When the belly is set, remove the
cramps, and cut the recess for the bottom nut or rest,
over which the tail-band or mainbrace passes. With the
dividers opened to ⅝ in., make a dot close inside the
purfling at each side of the centre joint, and with a knife
and small straight-edge cut out the oblong piece of the
belly thus described, and fit a piece of ebony ₁⁵₆ in.
square into the recess. When set, curve and file the
ebony to the same sweep as the belly round it, and
at ¼ in. from each end curve it down to the belly. The
" box " is now made, and begins to look like a fiddle.

The neck is next wanted, and the block from which it
is made is a piece of sycamore 10½ in. long, 2 in. broad,
and 2½ in. deep. The 2 in. side should be that nearest
the bark of the tree. Plane this side true, and call it
the "face." Next plane both 2½ in. sides true and with
the same bevel from the "face," and saw one end square
off. The block, when ready for use, should be 10¼ in.
long, 2½ in. deep, and 1⅝ in. on the face side, with an end
section like Fig. 68. It will now be convenient to make
a centre line along the face, square it down each end,
and continue with a straight-edge along the under side.
If the worker is fortunate enough to get a piece 2 in. wide
both top and bottom, his labour will be considerably
reduced, as it will be much easier to make the cuts true
or square. It will be of very great convenience if a neck
and scroll of good pattern are at hand for reference at
this stage of the work.

Fig. 69, the pattern of the neck and scroll, will be cut
out, as well as the other patterns, in zinc or thin wood.
The neck block being now ready, lay the pattern

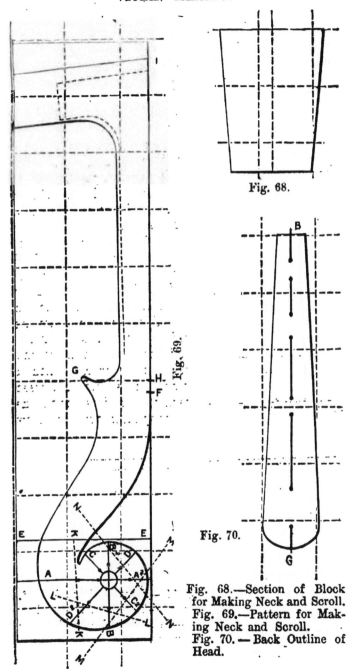

Fig. 68.

Fig. 69.

Fig. 70.

Fig. 68.—Section of Block
for Making Neck and Scroll.
Fig. 69.—Pattern for Mak-
ing Neck and Scroll.
Fig. 70. — Back Outline of
Head.

(Fig. 69) upon it, and trace round it with the marker pencilling afterwards ; next square the line A A ² across, and, $\frac{11}{32}$ in. from the top of this line, square from the end of the block the line B B ². The intersection of these lines gives the proper position, or centre, from which to describe the eye of the scroll, which is done by making a circle with the compasses opened to $\frac{5}{32}$ in. The line E E should be squared across ¾ in. from A. From a point midway between A ² and B and crossing the centre draw line C C², and from midway between A ² and B ² draw line D D ². Now prick through the dots on the lines in the following order : A, C, B ², D, A ², C ², B, D ², and then through the second or outer dot on A. When a proper curve is drawn between each of these dots, the outline of the spiral is complete. Now

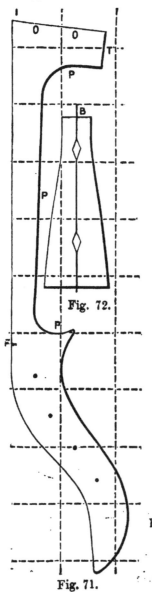

Fig. 72.

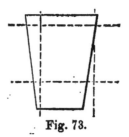

Fig. 73.

Fig. 71.—Front Outline of Head. Fig. 72.—Pattern of Neck. Fig. 73.—Pattern for Cutting Bevel for Shoulder.

Fig. 71.

square lines across the face at F H, and 5⅜ in. from
F the line I.

The outline may be cut out by a narrow band saw,
which is safer than the bow saw. If the neck is being made
from a piece like Fig. 68, a piece of deal sufficiently thick
to make the unmarked side lay square on the saw table
had better be glued on. After being sawed out, remove
the remnants of the strip, and mark this · side in a
corresponding way to the other side. The centre marks
will have been partially taken out by the saw, and the
line must now be continued all round the head from F
to G. Now square a line across the back at G. With
the compasses open ¾ in., set out that distance each side
of the centre line at I ; close the compasses to $\frac{7}{16}$ in., and
mark so much off each side of centre line at F, and with
a pencil and straight-edge make a line over the marks on
each side, but extend them to E. The sides thus marked
out should be sawn down, and then cut square off at E.

Trace the scroll outlines (Figs. 70 and 71) in their
places, as marked on the patterns. Open the compasses
to $\frac{3}{16}$ in., and draw them down each side of the head
from the end of line C to F ; one point of the compasses
will be at the side, and the other will mark out the
cheeks of the peg-box, which, being thus described or
marked, should at once be cut out with gouges and
chisels. When this has been done, file the cheeks clean
and square. Now fasten the neck edgeways in the vice,
and with a dove-tail saw or fine tenon saw cut down
just outside the lines K K, L L, M M, N N, but not so
deep as to cut into the lines marked from Figs. 70 and
71). Next saw at right angles with these cuts, and
along the marks made from Figs. 70 and 71.

The rough wood is now taken off, and with gouges of
various shapes it should now be possible, constantly re-
ferring to the model, to carve out a respectable scroll.
Afterwards the head should be scraped and glasspapered,
and sponged over with cold water ; this will throw
up the defects. When it is quite dry, gauge, with the
compasses opened $\frac{1}{16}$ in., lines all round the head and

scroll. Between the gauge mark and the centre line, from G round to C, the hollows should next be carved. With a fine file bevel off the edges all round the head and scroll as far as the compass lines ; now carefully glasspaper all over, leaving the edges of the bevels quite sharp. Much of this work will be saved if the neck and scroll is purchased already shaped.

The ebony finger-board will be bought ready made. With the veneer plane, make it true on the flat side, then mark a centre line along it. The "face" of the neck should also be toothed over with the same plane, and the centre line be freshened up.

For cutting the peg-holes, place the neck pattern (Fig. 72) flush with the neck and to the marks F and I, and trace firmly the lines O O, P P P, and also make the four dots where the peg-holes will have to be bored. Repeat the process in corresponding position on the other side of the neck, and with a tenon saw cut down O O, keeping square across centre mark at I. Now square the centre line down the face thus cut.

The finger-board should now be glued on (use only two or three drops of glue, as it must come off again before the fiddle is varnished), with the centre line coinciding with that on the neck, and the narrow end of the board touching the line H. The board being cramped fast with hand-screws, the nut should be glued on. It is a piece of ebony $\frac{1}{16}$ in. deeper than the thickest part of the narrow end of finger-board, $\frac{3}{16}$ in. wide and $1\frac{5}{8}$ in. long. Both nut and board being quite set, which they will do much more rapidly if made hot before they are glued, put the neck, board downwards, in the vice, and cut just outside line P P P with the bow saw. This done, file down to the line, using a small straight-edge to try the evenness of the neck, between the curves.

Remove the neck from the vice, and place the shoulder pattern (Fig. 73) with the top side close under, and even with the edges of the finger-board, and mark down both sides and across the bottom of pattern. With a gouge, followed with a broad chisel, cut to the lines last made, and also across the bottom at т (Fig. 72); along this face the centre line should next be squared. Fasten the neck in the vice, and cut off the parts which project over the finger-board, and with files make both the neck and nut even with the finger-board.

If the instrument has been made true to the lines, there will not be much difficulty in fitting on the neck. Place the neck with its back centre mark on the joint of the "tab", and the centre line of shoulder, coinciding with the joint of the belly. With a sharp knife make cuts slightly narrower than the shoulder in the end of the belly, and remove the neck. Extend the cuts to the edge of the purfling; lay a small straight-edge along the purfling, and cut out the rectangular piece of the belly between the shoulder-marks. Again put the neck in position, and with a very fine point trace the sides of the shoulder on the ribs, and cut through these lines into the block. With a ⅜ in. chisel cut the block down to the belly, proceeding very carefully and frequently trying the neck until the true position is obtained. This must be tested by looking along the sides of the finger-board and between the sound-holes, up the back joint and along the centre line of the head, and along the edges of the back, with which the eye of the scroll should be in line. Now mark the shape of the tab on the back of the shoulder.

The neck should next, with gouges, rasp, and files, be rounded to a rather oval shape, and then well glass-papered. Then the peg-holes can be bored with a ³⁄₁₆ in. bit, from outside each cheek, with a wedge or block inside the peg-box to make it solid. Now run the taper bit through the holes as a finish. The holes nearest the finger-board should taper from left to right, the next two from right to left, and so on. Now "size" the shoulder, and glue the neck in its place. In a few hours wash the fiddle over to remove all glue and dirt, and when dry, finish the "tab" and give a final rub with fine glasspaper, and the violin will then be finished in the "white."

CHAPTER IV.

VARNISHING AND FINISHING VIOLINS.

Low class violins are French polished or cheaply spirit varnished; but high-grade instruments, and most of those made by the old masters, are of oil-varnish finish. The process of oil-varnishing is a tedious one (extending over several weeks), owing to the time that must elapse between the application of the several coats of varnish to allow of thorough drying, the last coat having to be sufficiently hard to admit it to stand grinding down and polishing with rottonstone, etc.

A convenient process of varnishing violins and violoncellos is as follows :—The instrument is prepared by repeated glasspapering and damping until a dead smooth surface is obtained, quite free from scratches. It is not usual to stain violins, as a much finer effect is got by incorporating the colour with the varnish. Therefore, dilute 4 parts of copal varnish with 1 part (by measure) of turpentine, and heat it quite hot, being careful not to let it catch fire. Go over the entire violin with this with a stiff brush, and rub in as much as it will take at one coat; this will not be much if the wood was well finished. When the wood is quite filled, make a pad of cotton-wool, done up in a fine cotton or linen rag, moisten this with turpentine, and clean the surfaces of the violin as rapidly as possible; then put on a coat of spirit varnish made by dissolving 2 oz. of gum sandarach, two tablespoonfuls of Venice turpentine, and 2 oz. of bleached shellac in ½ pint of methylated spirit; the solution is coloured to the tone required by adding varying proportions of infusions of 2 oz. of red sanders wood and 2 oz. of turmeric respectively in two half pints of methylated spirit; filter through cotton-wool or fine muslin. This elastic spirit varnish gives the violin the warm amber colour so much sought for. Lay on the varnish carefully with a large, round, camel-hair brush, avoiding streaks, and not going twice over the same place. It will dry very quickly, and a coat may be put on daily till the desired colour is reached; rub down with finely sifted pumice-powder and water and a woollen rag after every third coat. When a good body of varnish is on, the surface must be rubbed down with the pumice-powder till the varnish is dull and smooth all over; the pumice is then thoroughly washed off. The final polish is obtained with tripoli and water, or crocus and linseed oil, on a rag, as before. After this is cleaned off, a brisk rub with the heel of the hand will give a surface like glass.

The above instructions are applicable also to re-varnishing an old violin; but then it is necessary, in the preliminary papering process, entirely to remove all traces of the old varnish. When that has been done, the work is identical with the above.

The process described above is probably the most convenient for the amateur violin maker, but the following, too, is easy, and has been warmly recommended : Place a small quantity of Howard's essential oil of turpentine in a cup, and put this in a water bath on a gas stove or other gentle source of heat. Then carefully dissolve as much gamboge as the oil will take up, and then lay a coat on the violin. In three hours, the first coat being dry, apply another coat of the same varnish. Two days afterwards the varnish will be quite hard—a beautiful yellow; the grain should not have risen, and will be quite bright. Having a good foundation, now apply coat after coat of varnish composed of the saturated alcoholic solutions of dragon's blood, sandarach, and benzoin (rubbing each coat down with wet pumice powder on a piece of oiled felt), until the varnish is quite solid and brilliant.

E

Although, as has been said, the colour generally is incorporated with the varnish, it is quite possible, if desired, to stain the wood itself before applying the varnish. Water stains may be used without raising the grain if the wood is first wiped over with raw linseed oil, either clear or red.

A black wavy grain appearance may be imparted by well rubbing with vegetable black and oil previous to applying varnish.

When oil varnishes are used throughout, the process resembles the second one described above ; two coats of the gamboge and turpentine are applied, followed by applications of oil varnish on alternate days.

A method of obtaining a rich brown colour is to use a solution of ½ oz. of permanganate of potash in 1 pt. of water. The work may be oiled first, the stain then applied and well rubbed in by means of a soft piece of rag. By this means the stain and oil will amalgamate and so prevent the grain rising. A slight tinge of red in the varnish will then give that ruddy tone so much desired.

A few recipes for violin varnishes may conveniently be given here. There is no better spirit varnish for the purpose than that given on p. 64. The preparation of suitable oil varnish requires special apparatus, and is therefore quite beyond the powers of amateurs. Suitable varnish that has been specially prepared for violins can be obtained at or through most large music shops. However, a recipe which has been recommended is :—Dissolve 3 oz. of copal and ⅔ pt. of pale drying oil in 1 gill of turpentine ; bismarck brown dissolved in methylated spirit will give a stain of dark orange red colour.

. The term amber varnish suitable for high-grade violins is often misleading. The high degree of finish that is seen on the better class of violins, and known as amber varnish finish, is not always produced by a varnish of which amber forms the basis. Generally the term means that the instruments have been finished a golden or amber colour ; and this result may be gained by using the spirit varnish given on p. 64, or an oil varnish.

Real amber oil varnish produces a most superior finish. It does not, of course, create tone, but it mellows and softens it remarkably. The objection to it from the worker's point of view is that it is generally slow-drying. It is important that each coat of varnish should be dry before the next is applied, and with a slow-drying preparation the worker's impatience is apt to get the better of him, and this, coupled with an anxiety to use the instrument again, accounts for many failures, which would not be so likely to occur when using a quick-drying preparation like spirit varnish. Amber oil varnish, as purchased, may be safely used if the directions given with the bottle are carefully followed. The Cremona amber oil varnish made by the late James Whitelaw, 496, St. George's Road, Glasgow, was the best known preparation of its kind. It was made in nine different shades of colour, from pale amber yellow to dark ruby, through intermediate shades of brown, orange, and red. One bottle, sufficient for one violin, cost about four shillings. Should the worker care to go to the great trouble of preparing amber oil varnish he should procure some broken amber from a pipe maker. Fill a test tube about 8 in. long one-fourth full of amber chips, and heat over a spirit flame till the amber froths up and finally liquefies into a brownish oily fluid. To this add about twice as much boiled linseed oil which has been separately heated. Simmer gently till a little taken out on the end of a wire can be drawn out into a fine thread on being touched with the finger. Allow it to cool a little, and add 1 part of pure turpentine. After cooling, it is ready for use ; three coats are sufficient to give a good deep colour. Before putting on this oil varnish, the violin should be sized with an alcoholic solution of gamboge. The oil varnish should be made in the open air, as there is considerable danger from fire during the process. Amber pipe-stems may be used for making the varnish if they are first thoroughly cleaned with spirits of turpentine.   Amber varnish should be permitted to dry surface hard at a temperature of 90° F., but may be allowed to harden at a much less temperature, say about 65° F.   Should the grain rise, rub down with No. 0 glasspaper.

Oil varnishes generally improve or mature with age, but are apt to thicken.   When this occurs the varnish should not be thinned down with an excessive quantity of turpentine, or the brilliancy and elasticity of the varnish will be lost.   Place the varnish in a suitable metal vessel, and heat over a fire to about 200° F., 1 part of turpentine (American) being added to 18 parts of varnish.   When the varnish possesses poor drying properties, the finest quality of terebine obtainable should be used instead of turpentine.   The quantity stated should not be exceeded, or the work will crack and lose its durability.

To remove unsatisfactory varnish from a violin, well rub it with flour emery or finest-grade pumice-stone powder moistened with water and applied with a woollen cloth.   With care, the top coats of varnish may thus be removed without injuring the under coat or spoiling the colour, or by continued rubbings the whole of the varnish can be removed until, with fine-grade glasspaper to smooth down the grain, a clean white surface is left.   Care must be taken to avoid excess of water likely to soften the glue joints.   Generally it is not advisable to remove old varnish when it is merely a case of matching repairs.   Repaired goods are usually doctored up by equalising the colour.   First rub the bare places with Venetian red and raw linseed oil; then take a small quantity of white hard spirit varnish or transparent polish and dragon's blood, and apply several coats to the light places.   Should the tone thus gained be too glaring, other colouring substances may be added, such as may be obtained by bismarck brown and red sanders;or pigments, as vandyke brown, amber, yellow ochre, or black.   When the colour has been equalised and a fair body of varnish laid on, allow it to get quite hard ; then

smooth down with very fine glasspaper and linseed oil,
and bring up the polish again by well rubbing with
jewellers' rouge and oil; finishing off with wheat flour
and the palm of the hand.

The art of imparting an aged appearance to a violin
without impairing its tone is not a very desirable one,
and can be acquired only by experience and a knowledge
of the chief characteristics of violins of the old school.
Using coloured varnish of various tones, holding the
violins in a smoky flame, sprinkling them with spirits or
liquid ammonia, scratching and bruising the varnished
surface, sprinkling the softened surface with powdered
resin and shaking a mixture of sand and carbon in the
inside, are all dodges used with more or less effect.
The *f* holes must also be indented so as to give the
sound-post the appearance of having been frequently
set, and due regard must be paid to the colour of the
instrument so that it shall accord with the varnish used
by the maker whose goods it is intended to represent.

Returning to the violin whose construction has been
described in the previous chapter, it should be varnished,
with the exception of the "handle" part of the neck,
and when the varnish is perfectly hard it will be ready
to have the neck cleaned. This done, glue the finger-
board on the neck again—this time quite fast. When it
is set, wash all dirt and glue from the neck, and polish
it up with the finest glass-paper and linseed oil. Take
care not to injure the varnish in doing this. With a
fine rat-tail file cut in the nut the four grooves in which
the strings are to lie. Mark the positions of the outer
grooves ⅛ in. from each end of the nut, and, with the
spring dividers, divide the intervening space into three
portions. Make all the grooves free from sharp edges,
which would cut the strings. Free the peg-holes from
varnish, and file a set of pegs to fit.

The bridge should be fitted to its position : between
the V's of the sound-holes. The feet could be cut with
a No. 1 gouge (see Fig. 22, p. 17). The top of the bridge
should have nearly the same curve as the finger-board

but should be about $\frac{3}{16}$ in. higher than the place at which
a line along the top of the finger-board would terminate
if extended to the bridge. The bridge will also need to
be made a trifle thinner towards the top. Make four
very shallow grooves with the file for the strings to lie
in. Fasten a piece of strong gut into the tail-piece, of
such length that when the loop is placed in the groove
of the end pin the tail-piece is brought close to the
bottom nut or rest.

The sound-post should now be set in position; but,
as remarked in the earlier part, there may be some
difficulty in deciding which is the best place for it, and
this can only be tested when the instrument is strung
up. This can now be done. First, put the fourth or G
string in the left-hand slit of the tail-piece, and through
the peg nearest the finger-board; the first or E string
is the next in order, then the third; and lastly the second
string. Whilst the strings are quite slack, set the bridge
in position, and screw the strings steadily up to pitch,
alternately fourth and first, second and third, meanwhile observing that the bridge does not pull forward.
Then the tone can be tried.

CHAPTER V.

DOUBLE BASS VIOLIN, AND A VIOLONCELLO.

THIS chapter will give drawings and sizes of a double bass violin. The proportions adopted by different makers vary a little, and are not so definitely fixed as the proportions of small violins ; those given here were taken from instruments of the average size, sometimes called a three-quarter double bass.

The number of strings is also a matter of taste, a good number of the old three-stringed basses having been altered to four strings, but the three-stringed instrument is still made.

In order to save giving a multiplicity of figures and sizes, the diagrams here presented have been lined off in 1-in. squares. Front and side views of the double bass are shown by Figs. 74 and 75, whilst a diagram showing the position of the bass-bar, sound-holes, back-bars, blocks, corner blocks, and end blocks is presented by Fig. 76. In order to lay off the outline full size, take a large sheet of cardboard, or several joined together, or thin boards jointed up, and line it out in 1-in. squares, then follow the lines of the diagram through the corresponding squares on the board, which will give a full-sized working drawing.

A half-model will be sufficient for the outline, as it can be reversed, which will ensure the outline being symmetrical. It is difficult to believe that Stradivarius made his outlines purposely unsymmetrical ; if he did, his example should not be followed in this matter.

The length of the string from where it leaves the nut to where it rests on the bridge is usually about 42 in. in this size of bass. If a full-sized orchestral bass is wanted this part of the string should measure 46 in., and all the

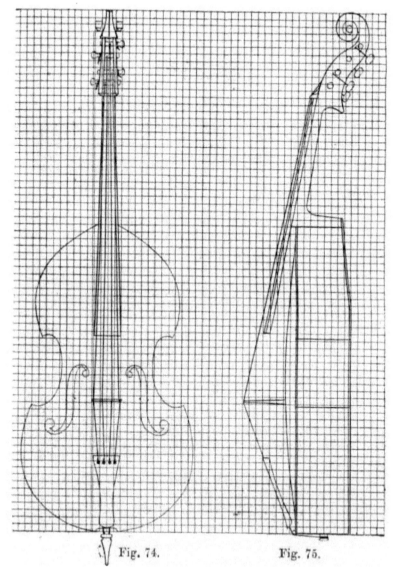

Fig. 74.   Fig. 75.

Figs. 74 and 75.—Front and Side Views of Double
Bass Violin.

other dimensions must be increased in proportion. The easiest way to arrive at this will be to make on the drawing-board each square $\frac{42}{46}$ in.—that is to say, mark off 46 in. and divide it into forty-two parts with compasses, and line off the board into squares of that size. When the length of the string from bridge to nut

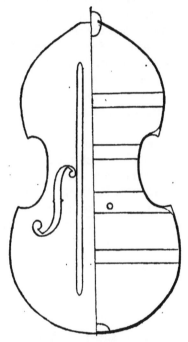

Fig. 76.—Diagram Showing Position of Bass-bar, Sound-holes, etc.

is 42 in. as above, the length of the neck between curves at the back is 15 in.

The back of the double bass may be made of plane-tree or maple, and may be planed to $\frac{3}{16}$ in. thick all over. This and all the other wood must be thoroughly seasoned and quite dry. The back is quite flat, excepting for a bend at the shoulder, which is shown in Fig. 75. It is made by cutting in half way from the inside with a tenon

saw, filling up the saw-kerf with glue, and wetting the
outside with warm water. There are four cross-bars
glued on the inside of the back to strengthen it, each
$\frac{1}{2}$ in. thick, preferably of Swiss pine. They are rounded
away on the top at the edges.

The correct positions of these bars can be got by
measuring Fig. 76 and comparing with the 1-in. scale
in Figs. 74 and 75. The breadth of the three narrow bars
is 2 in. ; the bar nearest the neck covers the saw-kerf at
the bend of the back, and the bar on which the sound-
post rests is 3 in. broad. The rims are made of the
same kind of wood as the back, and are $\frac{3}{8}$ in. thick.
They are bent by heat in the same manner as violin ribs,
and made up with a pine lining at the edges to about
$\frac{3}{16}$ in. thick.

The corner, neck, and tail blocks of the double bass
should be of Swiss pine, with the grain at right angles to
that of the ribs. The belly should also be of Swiss pine.
It may be left almost $\frac{3}{4}$ in. thick in the centre under the
bridge, and thinned away to nearly $\frac{1}{4}$ in. towards the
edges. The rise is generally about $1\frac{3}{4}$ in., measuring from
the back of the belly. The positions of the bass-bar and
sound-post are seen at Fig. 76. In a four-stringed
instrument, the distance between the centres of the
strings at the bridge may be $1\frac{1}{2}$ in., at the nut it may be
about $\frac{9}{16}$ in. The height of the bridge is usually about
7 in. ; its position is directly opposite the notches of
the f holes, provided these in their turn are properly
placed.

Drawings for a violoncello can easily be prepared from
the violin diagrams given on previous pages. The
differences are wholly a matter of dimensions. For a
full-sized violoncello make the length of body, exclusive
of button, 29 in. ; width across lower part, 17 in. ; width
across waist, $9\frac{1}{2}$ in. ; and the width across the upper part,
$13\frac{1}{2}$ in. The rough blocks for the back and belly would
be about 3 in. to 4 in. high at the centre joint, but much
depends on the model selected to build from. The ribs
should be worked out to about $\frac{1}{8}$ in. thick.

Instructions on making violins apply equally to violoncellos and double basses, dimensions, of course, excepted.

For making a violoncello, plane-tree or maple can be used for the back. Swiss pine is much the best for the belly, but if yellow pine is used the thickness should be slightly increased. The Swiss pine should be cut on the quarter, and jointed down the middle; if not jointed, use a middle-cut board. Sycamore is used for the ribs.

Several sound-posts should be made and tried, and the one used that gives the best results. Begin with one having a diameter just admitting it through the sound-holes, then trying those with smaller diameters. The proper place for the sound-post is about $\frac{1}{4}$ in. behind the right foot of the bridge. See that it stands quite upright, and that its fibres or grain are at right angles with the grain of the belly.

There is no arbitrary height for the bridge, as this should be specially fitted to each 'cello; $3\frac{1}{4}$ in. may be found suitable. For the best results a 'cello of heavy build would require a slightly higher bridge than one of lighter make. A rough guide, however, is to adjust the height so that the A string is about $\frac{7}{16}$ in. from the finger-board at the nut, and $\frac{5}{16}$ in. at the broad end of the finger-board; the C string about $\frac{3}{32}$ in. at the nut, and $\frac{3}{8}$ in. at the other end.

The making and fitting of a bass-bar for a violoncello is a job for which a charge of 10s. or 12s. is often made. But the worker can do it quite well at home. To make the bar, get a piece of straight-grained Swiss pine as old as possible, provided it be sound; cut it 21$\frac{3}{4}$ in. long by 1$\frac{1}{4}$ in. by $\frac{1}{2}$ in., plane it to the above size, then bevel it from $\frac{1}{2}$ in. thickness to $\frac{5}{16}$ in. Take the centre of the bar and make a mark on the $\frac{5}{16}$ in. edge; take the spoke-shave and taper to both ends from 1$\frac{1}{4}$ in. with a nice gradual, somewhat hollow, sweep to $\frac{1}{4}$ in.; round over the thin edge and glass-paper it well. At this point the bass-bar is supposed to be ready for gluing into the belly; consequently, in roughing it out, the worker had

better leave it at least ¼ in., as he has now the worst
part of the job to face, namely, scribing it to the belly.
To make a proper job the belly must be taken off to get
a clean joint between the bass-bar and the inside of the
belly. Set a pair of compasses to, say, ½ in. apart
between the legs ; run one leg along the belly, the other
along the side of the bass-bar ; plane parallel with the
line cut on the side of the bass-bar, and a clean joint
will result. The bass-bar must be planed on the thick
or ½ in. edge. Fig. 77 is a side elevation of the bass

Fig. 77.

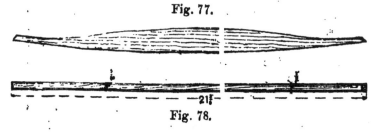

Fig. 78.

Figs. 77 and 78.—Bass-bar for Violoncello.

bar, and Fig. 78 is a plan of the edge which is glued to
the belly of the 'cello. After it is fitted as stated above,
take a shaving off the two ends so that when gluing the
bar down it will be necessary in order to make a close
joint to put a handscrew at both ends of the bar to bed
the joint ; this is called gluing the bass-bar in with a
spring, which is considered to be the proper way to fix
bass-bars of violins, violas, 'cellos, and bass violins, or
double bass. To take the belly off, take a thin-bladed
table-knife and insert it between the plate of the belly
and the edge of the ribs, and carefully work round the
'cello till the plate is off. The belly is then ready to
receive the bass-bar. The foregoing sizes are correct for
a ¾-size 'cello ; for a full-size 'cello it would, of course,
be necessary slightly to enlarge the bass-bar.

CHAPTER VI.

JAPANESE ONE-STRING VIOLINS.

A ONE-STRING violin is a sweet-toned instrument at all times, even when made from a soap-box. One form of Japanese fiddle may be cheaply constructed by using for the body the half of a large cocoanut shell. The neck is of sycamore or similar straight-grained wood, and passes through the cocoanut shell, so protruding that it forms a button to take the tailpiece. The finger-board is a strip of ebony carefully glued to the neck. A thin piece of deal forms the top of the body, and has a sound-hole cut in it. Both the shell and the top must be carefully dressed to fit perfectly true when glued together. When a coat of the best varnish has been applied the instrument is ready for stringing.

The above form of fiddle is liable to slip when held between the knees, but the octagon or hexagon shape has been recommended as being free from this defect.

A one-string violin with a hexagonal body is shown in plan by Fig. 79, and in side elevation by Fig. 80, reproduced one-quarter size, and the instructions here given will enable anyone to make a very serviceable instrument. Glue only is used for the joints. The body of the violin is 9 in. in diameter inside, and yellow pine is used for both belly and back. The sides are $\frac{3}{32}$ in. thick by 1½ in. high, and are mitred at the corners.

The arm or handle is cut from good straight-grained pitch-pine. Those who are proficient in the use of woodworking tools will no doubt be able to lay a strip of ebony A about ⅛ in. thick along the top of the handle or arm, from the neck to a projection of 3½ in. past the shoulder, which butts up against the fiddle body ; but as an alternative a short piece may be fitted in and glued.

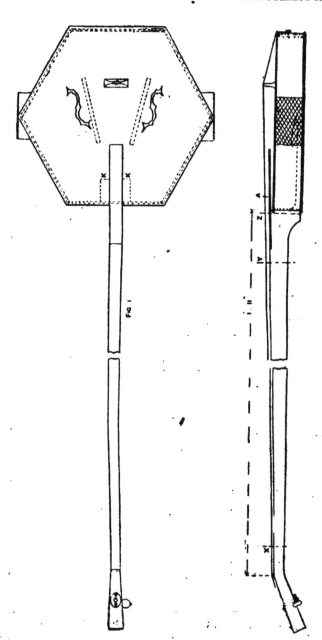

Figs. 79 and 80.—Plan and Side Elevation of Japanese Violin.

The handle is screwed to one of the sides, and has an extension which is glued down to the bottom half-way as shown in Figs. 80 and 81, the latter figure being a half-size detail of the body, showing the method of framing up. Sections at x, y, and z (Fig. 80) are given in Figs. 82 to 84.

The length of the neck of the violin should be about 3 in. to 3½ in., and the peg on the machine head should go through half-way between the beginning of the finger-board and the end of the neck. The top of the neck is expanded out square at the end to give a better finish, and a machine head, which can be obtained at any music-dealer's, is used. In fitting the machine head, all that is required to be done is to drill a small round hole for the barrel to project through, and to screw on the plate (see Figs. 85 and 86). An ordinary violin peg is suitable, with careful boring of the hole, so as not to split the head. To secure the string to the body a small button is screwed to the bottom side of the body (see Figs. 87 and 88), those sold for handles for fretwork cupboards being very suitable. A small square of wood is glued on the inner side to form a better hold for the screw. The handle is at an angle to the body, so as to keep the bridge a good height. The wire string should be about ⅛ in. from the finger-board at the bridge end, and ₁₆ in. at the neck end. All the wood must be well glass-papered. The glue used should be thin.

In putting the parts together, begin with the bottom of the violin, and lay all the sides on, having the handle already screwed on. Two small triangular brackets k (Fig. 79) are glued each side of the arm where it comes in the body, to strengthen up the side and keep the handle or arm from bending when the string is being tightened. Then glue a small sound-post at a distance of one-third up the body from the bottom end, about ₁₆ in. in diameter, and just high enough to keep the top from fitting down on the sides. The dotted lines under the sound-holes in Fig. 79 represent two small banking-up pieces for strengthening the face of the

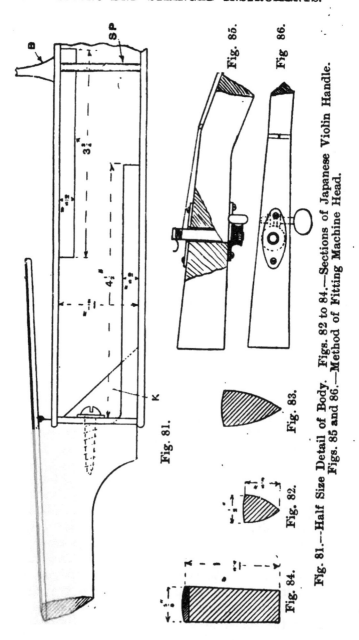

Fig. 81.—Half Size Detail of Body. Figs. 82 to 84.—Sections of Japanese Violin Handle. Figs. 85 and 86.—Method of Fitting Machine Head.

violin body ; they are ¼ in. square wood strips, about 3½ in. long, and are glued on. The strip of wood shown in Fig. 81 is one of the two banking-up pieces shown dotted in Fig. 79, lying close to the F holes or sound-holes. The

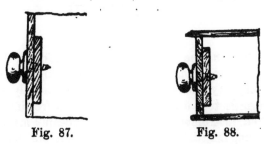

Fig. 87.   Fig. 88.

Figs. 87 and 88.—Button for Securing Spring.

top is fixed on by clamping all round, and then allowing it to set hard. Two knee-caps (Figs. 89 and 90) are then cut to shape to give a good hold of the violin when playing, and a small chequer-work cut in. Then rub down with glass-paper, and varnish with a good oil varnish ; or finish off with water stain and French polish. The repeated applications of glass-paper and polish will make it look quite handsome if time is taken

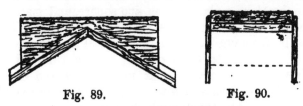

Fig. 89.   Fig. 90.

Figs. 89 and 90.—Detail of Knee Caps.

to do it. A wire G string, such as those sold for banjos, is the best kind to use, the open string being tuned to A. The correct position for the bridge is obtained by trying in various places till the tone seems purest.

It may be necessary to point out that this instrument is held between the knees, like an ordinary violoncello, and is played with a bow.

CHAPTER VII.

MANDOLINE MAKING.

CONSIDERING the popularity of the mandoline, the dearth of home-made instruments is surprising, especially as the majority of cheap bought ones are usually very poor as regards tone and correctness of the fretting. A flat-backed instrument is easily and cheaply made, as the following instructions show. A mandoline made in the manner described in this chapter has been in use for many years, and has been played in public, both as a solo instrument and by the leader of a mandoline band, and it compares favourably with many high-priced instruments for quality and evenness of tone. More-over, there is no sign of defect at the place where so many instruments give way, namely, at the joint of the handle and the body.

First obtain a piece of well-seasoned hard wood, oak or walnut, free from knots, and cut to size, 14 in. by 2¼ in. by 1½ in. ; plane it true and square, and mark it out as follows :—At A (Fig. 91) draw a line on the 1½ in. side 5¼ in. from one end, and another B 3¼ in. from the other end. From c to D draw a line, c being 1 in. and D ½ in. from the top edge. Next join D to E and draw A G parallel, and connect H to I. Then cut away the darker portions. On the top, which is the 2¼ in. side, draw a line down the centre, then draw lines A and B (Fig. 92) corresponding with A and B (Fig. 91) ; and on A mark the points c, each ⅝ in. from the centre line, and on B mark the points D, each ¾ in. on either side of the centre line. Join c D, continuing the lines as shown, and cut away the darker portions as before to produce the handle in the rough. The neck between c and D (Fig. 91) should then be rounded and the whole smoothed with sand-paper

Next obtain a cheese tub, and from the best and
smoothest part cut a strip 2¼ in. wide and 30½ in. long
for the rim, and trim it down to 2½ in. wide. This, of
course, is already in a circular form, and will bend to the
required shape if steamed a little. For the bending,

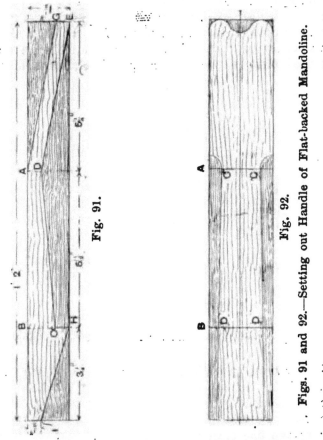

Fig. 91.

Fig. 92.

Figs. 91 and 92.—Setting out Handle of Flat-backed Mandoline.

make an inside mould of thick wood, shaping it something like Fig 93, and making it 9½ in. long from A to B,
3½ in. across at A, and 7½ in. across at C, the widest part,
4½ in. from B. Cut also two ¾-in. holes (shown in Fig. 93)
to facilitate the removal of the mould from the body of
the instrument. Next cut a piece of wood ⅜ in. thick to

Fig. 94, which, for convenience sake, may be called the partition. It must be of the same width as the mould at its narrow end A (Fig. 93), with the ends bevelled slightly to continue the curve of the mould as at A B (Fig. 95). The piece cut away fits the handle closely. The height of the partition is 2½ in., the same as the rim, which can now be steamed and bent round the mould, with the partition held close to the flat end of the mould, and in a perfectly upright position. The ends of the rim, when fixed to the partition, must be quite level, and this can

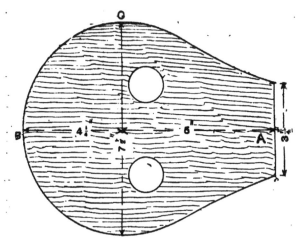

Fig. 93.—Inside Mould for Flat-backed Mandoline.

be ensured by marking a point exactly half way round the rim, and making a corresponding mark half way round the mould, and, when bending, putting the two marks together. The rim can be fixed and kept in shape by two fine brass screws on each side, screwed through the rim into the partition. When the wood is dry these screws can be withdrawn a little, and some hot glue run in the joint, the screws being tightened up again. Probably it will be found that the protruding ends of the rim are too close together for the handle to slip in easily, and that the rim just below the partition is not

quite close to the mould ; however, this will close up
when the handle is forced between the ends of the rim,
the wood springing to bring it to the required shape.
Shave off the ends of the rim to a knife-edge from the
inside to make a close joint with the handle, which can
then be placed in position, the ends of the rim reaching
to B (Fig. 92). Fix the handle with good glue and fine
screws, both through the rim and into the side, and
through the top into the partition, being careful not to
split the rim. Take every precaution to get the handle
in line with the rim, the handle being ¼ in. higher than
the top edge of the rim, as shown in Fig. 96. Also see
that a line drawn down the centre of the handle would,
if continued, pass through the centre of the body.

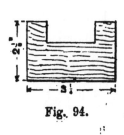

Fig. 94.

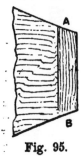

Fig. 95.

Figs. 94 and 95.—Partition for Flat-backed Mandoline.

Then, from rather soft wood, with a straight, even
grain, but no knots, and ¼ in. thick, cut the belly and
the back, which must be cut to fit the shape of the body.
The piece for the belly must be cut to fit the lower end
of the handle, so that in position the face of the handle
and the belly shall be quite flush.

The back may be 1 in. shorter at the neck end, and
the rim cut away to meet it, the resulting corner being
afterwards covered with a flat piece of wood for finish.
This is illustrated at A (Fig. 96), which shows the back
glued into position and fixed with hardwood pegs or
fine brass brads. The mould can be removed as soon as
the back is properly fixed; in removing ease it out gently.

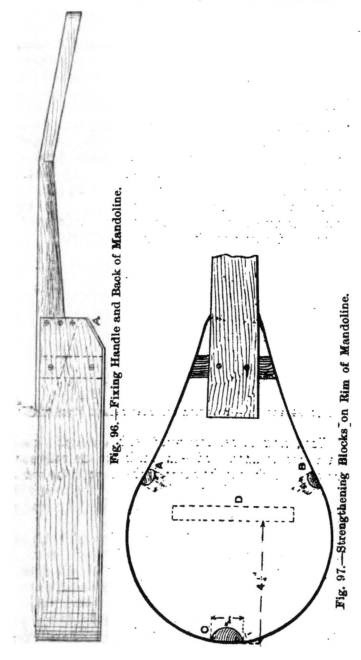

Fig. 96.—Fixing Handle and Back of Mandoline.

Fig. 97.—Strengthening Blocks on Rim of Mandoline.

Make two small blocks of wood ½ in. wide, and glue
them to the inside of the rim at A and B (Fig. 97), and
one 1 in. wide at C. All are shaped to fit close to the
rim and add to the strength. A thin strip is glued to
the inside of the front and one to the inside of the back,
about 4½ in. from the tail end of the body, as shown by
the dotted lines in Fig. 97.   Upright between these
strips is set a sound-post D, about ¼ in. to the right of
the centre of the body.   It must fit well between the
belly and back, and can be held upright in position by a
drop of glue whilst the front is fixed in position, after

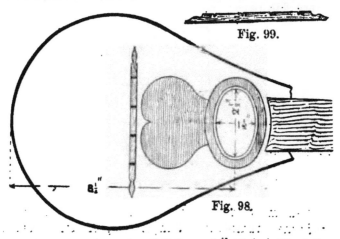

Fig. 99.

Fig. 98.

Fig. 98.—Position of Sound Holes and Bridge on Mandoline.
Fig. 99.—Mandoline Bridge.

which, of course, the pressure of the front and back will
keep it up.

Before attaching the belly, the inside of the body
should be cleaned off, and made smooth everywhere
with glass-paper, so as not to leave any rough or loose
parts likely to rattle or jar.   Then the inside should be
neatly lined with dark-coloured paper, as, the sound-hole
being rather large, the interior can be seen.   At this
stage any ornamentation to the front should be done.
A simple design of dark-cigar-box wood can be inlaid

round and below the sound-hole, leaving a light line round the edge of the hole, something like Fig. 98; anything more elaborate might appear rather out of place on this instrument.

The centre of the oval-shaped sound-hole, 1½ in. by 2½ in., is 8¼ in. from the tail end of the body (see Fig. 98). The hole should be cut and a straight bar glued right across the inside of the belly, close to the lower edge of the sound-hole. Then put the sound-post in position, and glue and fix the belly as for the back. Smooth everything with glass-paper, finishing off with very fine paper.

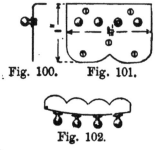

Fig. 100.   Fig. 101.

Fig. 102.

Figs. 100-102.—Tail-piece for Mandoline.

Next make the fingerboard of ⅛-in. walnut, cutting it to fit the handle and leaving it long enough to reach the sound-hole. This must be glued to the face of the handle, and will consequently stand ⅛ in. above the belly. An ebony nut, nicked to take the four pairs of strings, is fixed at the top end of the fingerboard, 17¾ in. from the tail end of the instrument.

In fretting the fingerboard much care must be taken. First find the place for fret No. 1 by dividing the distance from the bridge to the nut by eighteen, and making a mark on the fingerboard at this distance from the nut. For fret No. 2 measure as before, but from fret No. 1 to the bridge, instead of from the nut to the bridge ; divide by eighteen to get the distance of fret No. 2 from fret No. 1. Then measure

from fret No. 2 to the bridge, and divide again as
before for fret No. 3; and so on, until all the frets
are marked, the distance between the frets thus de-

Fig. 103.—American Mandoline with Machine Head.

creasing. Fret wire, which is sold for the purpose
by most musical instrument dealers, should be let in
by carefully making narrow cuts at the marks, and
hammering in the wire, which must be previously
cut to the proper lengths.

The bridge (Fig. 99), 5 in. long, should stand
·12¾ in. from the ebony nut, and can be made of
walnut. It must be high enough to raise the strings
about ⅛ in. above the belly of the instrument, and the
nicks for the outside pairs of strings should be 1½ in.
apart, the others being spaced equally.

A tail-piece (Figs. 100 to 102) of thin sheet brass,
1 in. by 1½ in. wide, with four knobs to hold the
looped ends of the strings, should be made and screwed
to the end of the instrument, so that the screws enter

Fig. 104.—Outside Mould for American Mandoline.

the block c (Fig. 97). A pleasing appearance is
presented if this tail-piece is made of a fancy pattern
and cut from German silver sheet. The final finishing
can now be done according to taste, but a good plan
is to stain the rim, back, and the handle to a dark
rosewood colour, leaving the belly white, and then to
French polish or varnish all over, with the exception
of the fingerboard, which should have a little oil
rubbed in.

The only thing now needed besides the strings is
the machine head, which it is advisable to buy ready

made at the place where the strings and fret wire
are bought. It will consist of two strips containing
the screws and pegs for holding the strings, and each
strip should be screwed to the under side of the flat
slope at the end of the handle, with the bone nuts protruding from the side, whilst the pegs for the strings
stick upwards through holes made in the wood to
receive them. (The usual shape of machine head is
shown in Fig. 103, which illustrates an American pattern
mandoline and gives all essential measurements ; this
instrument is made in the outside mould represented
by Fig. 104.)

A few mother-of-pearl dots, made from an old knife
handle or tops and backs of collar studs, should be let
into the fingerboard between the fourth and fifth, the
sixth and seventh, the ninth and tenth, and the eleventh
and twelfth frets, as this not only greatly improves
the appearance, but shows the most used positions at
a glance.

CHAPTER VIII.

GUITAR MAKING.

THIS chapter will give some hints on how to make a guitar, and will present illustrations of different models. .The form and dimensions of a full-size Spanish guitar are given in Fig. 105. The body and neck might with advantage be smaller than the sizes given if it is intended to tune up to concert pitch, as the strings on the large-sized instruments do not stand well if pulled right up to play with the violin, etc. Many different designs have been adopted by makers of guitar bodies, and the worker can either copy one of the designs here given, or can sketch one to his own fancy.

The guitar belly is made of Swiss or other pine, the sides and back of mahogany, rosewood, maple, satin-wood, or walnut, etc. The depth of the Spanish guitar illustrated is $3\frac{3}{4}$ in. at the lower end, tapering to $3\frac{1}{4}$ in. at the part where the neck joins the body. The depth is also a matter in which the worker may follow his own ideas; some instruments are made 3 in. or $3\frac{1}{2}$ in. in depth. The Andalusian model (Fig. 106) is made very shallow in comparison with the Spanish model (Fig. 105) —about 2 in. to $2\frac{1}{2}$ in. The French model is illustrated by Fig. 107; the American by Fig. 108; and Fig. 109 shows the Spanish lyre guitar. The following instructions apply more particularly to the Spanish guitar shown by Fig. 105.

The guitar can be built on an outside mould of the type shown by Fig. 104 (p. 90), or on an inside mould (Fig. 110). Draw a full-size design of the model on paper—half the pattern will do. Paste the drawing on a piece of thin wood, and cut it out to the marks. This produces the pattern of one half of the body. In

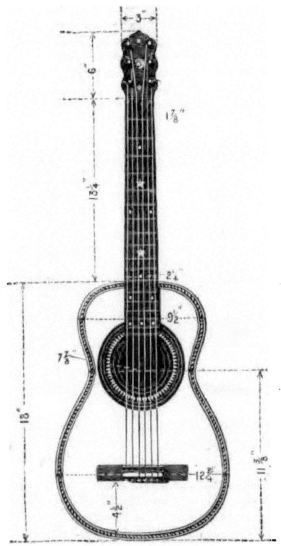

Fig. 105.—Spanish Guitar.

cutting out the pattern, allowance must be made for the thickness of the sides of the guitar, as they will be bent round the outside of the mould. The mould

can be made from a solid piece of wood of the right
thickness, or can be built up of two or three thicknesses
of wood glued together, according to the convenience of
the worker.　Get the mould cut out at a saw-mill
with a band or fret saw—the sides will be then nice and
square, and much better than if cut out with a hand
bow saw.　Failing the saw-mill, a bow saw must be

Fig. 106.—Andalusian　　　Fig. 107.—French
Guitar.　　　　　　　Guitar.

used afterwards, finishing the sides with a square and
spokeshave.　Cut out also the holes in the mould for
fixing the cramps.　The blocks, top and bottom, must be
fixed with a dab of glue in the recesses of the mould cut
out to receive them, and then worked off outside to the
shape of the mould.　The blocks can be loosened from
the mould with a thin table-knife when the back is
glued on.　The wood that is cut away from the outside
of the mould is kept and used for clamping blocks.

Spanish guitars are generally made with blocks glued to
the back and sides, and belly and sides, in place of
linings, placed at intervals of about ¾ in. all round. If
the guitar is made on the inside mould shown by
Fig. 110, grooves must be cut across the back of the
mould as indicated by the dotted lines, so that the three
stays can be let into the lining on the sides, and glued
before the back is fixed on.

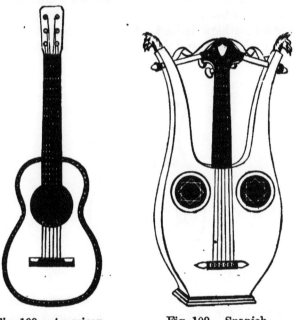

Fig. 108.—American   Fig. 109.—Spanish
Guitar.   Lyre-guitar.

In marking out the mould, make a line along the
centre of the wood ; lay the half pattern along the centre
line, mark the outline, turn over the pattern, still keeping the straightedge in line with the centre line, and
mark the other half of the outline. Both sides will then
be exactly alike.

The back can be made in one piece, or glued up with
a joint in the centre, or a piece of white or dark coloured

wood can be put between the joints to give the back a
better appearance. The maker must work and think
for himself in adding these finishing touches. The belly
and round the sound-hole can be purfled, or inlaid with
pearl or fancy woods, or left plain, as desired.

A bridge, to which the strings are fixed, is shown by
Fig. 111. It is very important that the bridge be very
firmly glued to the belly, using best quality fresh glue ;
if the bridge came away from the belly whilst the instrument was being played, it would give the performer
a very severe blow indeed. Use wood about ⅛ in. thick
for the back, belly, and sides. Mark where the bridge

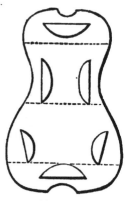

Fig. 110.—Inside Mould for Guitar.

will come on the drawing, and then measure from the
bridge to the top end of body where the neck joins on ;
this will give the exact length of neck to nut from the
body of the instrument. The twelfth fret should come
exactly above the junction of the fingerboard to body.
It is not of great importance if it does not do so, providing the frets are spaced in tune ; still, it is as well to
be as nearly correct as possible.

In setting the neck to the body, see that the face of
it is in a straight line with the face of belly ; or, if anything, the end where the pegs are ought to lie back a
trifle out of the straight line so as to bring the strings

nearer the fingerboard ; then they will not be so difficult to press down.

Fret wire can be had specially made, or plain brass or German silver can be used. Make saw-cuts across the fingerboard ; have the metal to fit in tightly, but not too tightly, or it will wedge the neck back out of truth, or the saw-cuts can be made easy, and the frets made hot and fixed in with shellac. File down the frets, using a straightedge to get them true, and do not let them project much above fingerboard ; take off the sharp edges, or they will cut the strings. The specially prepared fret wire will not want filing except at the ends.

It is very important that the neck and frets are nicely adjusted for comfort in playing. Use a piece of ebony, blackwood, or rosewood ¼ in. thick, for the

Fig. 111.—Guitar Bridge, showing Method of
Fastening Strings.

fingerboard. An ivory nut is unsuitable, as it. tends to cut the strings. A piece of wood is the best. Mark the principal positions with pearl dots or coloured wood, etc., as shown in Fig. 105 ; this system is a great help in playing. Many guitars are fitted with machine-made heads, but they are rather a bother. Nothing beats pegs for gut and silk strings, if they are properly fitted and the knack acquired of using them. If pearl positions are put in the fingerboard, fix them in ; file and glass-paper off before the frets are put in, marking the correct places from the fretting scale. They are much easier to do, and a better job can be made than by putting in after the frets are fixed.

An improved fingerboard can be applied to the guitar, mandoline, banjo, or any stringed instrument. The fingerboard is planed true, the frets are fixed in and filed off flush. Then the wood is filed back to a

G

little below the level of each fret, only just enough to allow the string to rest on the fret and vibrate without touching the wood in front. By this method it is claimed that the fingers can slide along the strings rapidly without catching against the frets.

To set out the fretting scale proceed as explained on p. 88 of the previous chapter.

The belly must have pine stays across fixed on to the sides, similar to the back, to support it. Put one of the stays near the bridge, which will help to take the strain off the belly, and one above and another below the sound-hole. The stays, instead of being planed off straight across the back, can be slightly arched from the side, to the centre, so that the back, when it is fixed on, will be convex.

Fingerboards on some guitars, instead of being made flat, are made convex, and the frets filed to the same shape.

CHAPTER IX.

BANJO MAKING.

THE making of a full-size six-string banjo will now be described. For the handle (Figs. 112 and 113) use a piece of walnut 2 ft. 9¼ in. long by 2½ in. square; this should be cut out roughly with a bow saw, and then finished to dimensions. The fingerboard A is of ebony ⅛ in. thick. The surface of the walnut handle is first made smooth; then, with an old saw blade, make a series of scratches. Do the same on one side of the ebony slip, and then glue the roughened surfaces together. The bottom part, as B, should have a radius ¼ in. larger than that of the bowl, and may be ¼ in. clear from the bowl when in position (Fig. 113). The ring and hoop then clear the handle. A piece of ivory or ebony C (Figs. 112 and 113) is glued in and projects ⅛ in. above the finger-board. Its grooves (see Fig. 114) are ¹⁄₃₂ in. deep, the sharp edges being removed. At E (Figs. 112 and 113) a tapering hole is made ¾ in. deep to fit the peg (Fig. 115). Five holes are also drilled at the top of the handle; these should taper from the underside, so that the pegs project ⅜ in. above the surface. If, when the strings are tightened, the pegs slip, a little powdered resin sprinkled on them will increase their holding power. Drill a hole at F (Figs. 112 and 113) and fit a piece of bone or ivory ¼ in. in diameter and ⅝ in. long tightly into this to project ¼ in. A small groove is filed across for the string to rest in.

The bowl is of oak, 2½ in. wide and ¼ in. thick. The ends should be thinned out for about 5 in. at each end, and roughened as before explained, then glued and clamped firmly together. When finished it should have a uniform thickness all round, the outside diameter

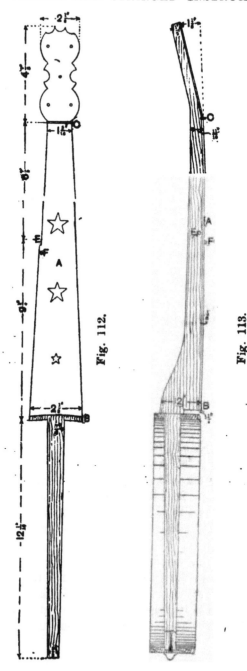

Fig. 112.

Fig. 113.

Figs. 112 and 113.—Front and Side Elevations of Handle of Banjo.

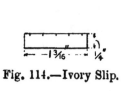

Fig. 114.—Ivory Slip.

Fig. 115.—
Peg.

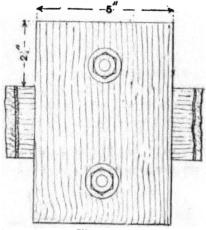

Fig. 116.

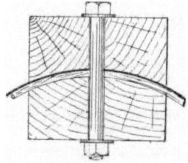

Fig. 117.
Figs. 116 and 117.—Wood Clamps for Making Banjo.

being 12₁ᵃ₆ in. The appearance of the instrument will
be improved if the outside of the bowl is covered with
a thin layer of veneer; polished rosewood looks well,
with bright nickel fittings. Get a slip of veneer a little

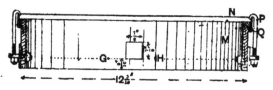

Fig. 118.—Banjo Bowl.

longer than the circumference of the bowl and 2⅝ in.
wide, and to glue this on cut two blocks of wood 2 in.
thick, 5 in. wide, by 7 in. long, to Figs. 116 and 117, the
radius of the curve and bowl being equal. Roughen the
bowl and glue about 5 in. of veneer to the bowl, and
clamp together with the two wood blocks. When
dry, unclamp the pieces, put on more glue, and proceed until complete.

When the bowl is finished, make a ¼-in. square hole
through where the two veneer ends meet, and scribe a

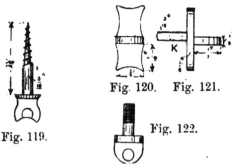

Fig. 120.   Fig. 121.

Fig. 119.

Fig. 122.

Fig. 119.—Screw for Banjo Handle.   Figs. 120-122.—
Clamping Bracket.

line all round as in Fig. 118. From the centre of this
hole, and on the scribed line, mark off twenty-three
divisions with the dividers; then drill twenty-two holes
either ₃⁄₁₆ in. in diameter, or according to size of clamping

screws used, beginning at G (Fig. 118), H being the last
hole. Put the handle through, and hold the end close
against the opposite side of the bowl; then put a
straightedge along the fingerboard. The handle and
the top of the hoop must be in the same plane. Mark
round the bottom of the handle with a sharp pencil, and
drill a $\frac{3}{16}$-in. hole through the centre of this square;
then cut the marked portion out with a chisel, making
it $\frac{1}{8}$ in. deep. The handle should fit tightly. The other
end of the bowl should butt against the shoulder, as
seen in Fig. 113, and is kept in position by a screw

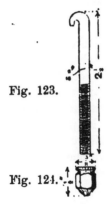

Fig. 123.

Fig. 124.

Figs. 123 and 124.—Clamping Screw and Nut.

(Fig. 119) with a coarse thread. This can be purchased
with the other fittings. A ring can then be made from
$\frac{3}{16}$-in. round brass rod, the ends being filed wedge shape
for about 1 in., and silver-soldered together. This hoop
must fit easily over the bowl.

The band that holds the parchment down is made as
follows :—File the ends of strip brass $\frac{9}{16}$ in. by $\frac{1}{16}$ in. as
before, and bend and silver-solder to an inside diameter
of $12\frac{7}{16}$ in. Make another ring, $\frac{1}{4}$ in. wide by $\frac{1}{16}$ in.
thick, to fit tightly inside the first one and flush all
round with the bottom edge, to which it is then firmly
soldered. Round off the inside edge, to prevent cutting the
parchment. Twenty-two brackets (Figs. 120 to 122) and

screws (Figs. 123 and 124) will now be required. The method of attachment is shown by Fig. 118. Fig. 125 shows another form of bracket, which is clamped to the bowl by means of a screw and washer from the inside; the hole in the centre of the large part is for the

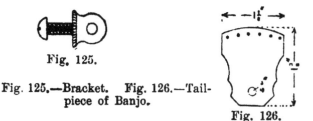

Fig. 125.

Fig. 125.—Bracket.   Fig. 126.—Tail-
piece of Banjo.

Fig. 126.

clamping screw to pass through. The bowl and handle should be French polished, but not the ebony finger-board ; a little fine sand- or glass-paper used on this will lay a smooth, even grain. Fasten the brackets inside the bowl with small nuts and washers.

When purchasing the parchment see that it is of a uniform thickness. Steep it in clean cold water just long enough to take out the stiffness ; then lay it on the bench on a clean sheet of paper. Now put the $\frac{3}{16}$-in. brass ring Q (Fig. 118) centrally on the parchment, and with a needle and cotton draw the ends over the ring, sewing near the edge from several points. Now place this on the bowl M (Fig. 118) with the edge of the parchment uppermost, and put the brass hoop N on this with its thicker edge downwards ; gently press this all

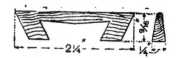

Fig. 127.—Banjo Bridge.

the way round, and put a clamp on here and there. When the hoop is in position, all the clamping screws P (Fig. 118) may be attached, just sufficient pressure being applied to bring the parchment tight ; leave the top of the

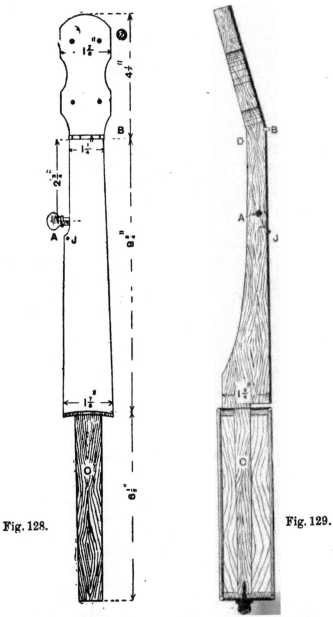

Fig. 128.

Fig. 129.

Figs. 128 and 129.—Front and Side Views of Handle
of Piccolo Banjo.

hoop $\frac{3}{16}$ in. above the top of the bowl. Now with pliers pull the ends of the parchment to remove all wrinkles, and put the whole aside till dry; then trim the edges of the parchment with a sharp penknife, cutting just below where the clamping screws grip the hoop. See that there is an even tension all round, the top of the hoop presenting a level appearance.

The tail-piece (Fig. 126) is of bone, ivory, or ebony, $\frac{3}{16}$ in. thick. The lower hole is for a long screw that passes through the head of the tail-piece screw, to which it is held by a small nut; it serves the purpose of keeping the strings and tail-piece in position.

The bridge (Fig. 127) is made from hard wood, as mahogany or ebony; some players prefer the bridge wider and not so high. Set into the fingerboard are three pearl stars, the holes for them being fretted out before gluing the ebony to the handle. The bridge is usually placed at 3 in. or 4 in. from the bottom of the bowl. Six pegs (Fig. 115) will complete the banjo; five of these have a $\frac{1}{16}$-in. hole drilled $\frac{1}{4}$ in. from the top through which the strings are passed, but in the lower peg for the thumb-string the hole is drilled near the centre.

A piccolo banjo is much smaller than the instrument just described, and it may have a metal bowl instead of a wooden one. The making of such a banjo will now be discussed.

The handle of a piccolo banjo may be made from a piece of walnut, 1 ft. 9 in. long by 2 in. square, as shown by Figs. 128 and 129. Four holes are drilled through at the top, and then opened with a taper bit from the under side to take the pegs (Fig. 130). These are $\frac{1}{16}$ in. in diameter at the top, tapering to $\frac{3}{8}$ in. at the bottom, the shank being $1\frac{1}{2}$ in. long. Another hole is drilled at the side, as shown at A (Figs. 128 and 129), to take the peg for the thumb-string. A piece of ebony or bone is let into the top of the handle, as seen at B, and should be $\frac{1}{8}$ in. wide by $\frac{1}{4}$ in. thick, with four slots filed across to keep the strings in position. The end c of the handle is cut away as shown, and may be 1 in. wide at the top

tapering to ⅞ in. and ⅝ in. thick. The back is then shaped
as seen by Fig. 129, and rounded. At the top it is ⅜ in.
thick, at D ¾ in., and 1¾ in. thick at the bottom.

In Fig. 129 the black line represents an ebony finger-
board glued to the face of the handle ; this is not
necessary, but improves the finish of the instrument. If
the ebony fingerboard is to be used, first plane the face
of the handle true ; then before gluing them together
scratch the two surfaces that are to be united, as this
makes a stronger joint ; firmly clamp them together
until dry. The face is then finally sandpapered and

Fig. 130.—Peg.

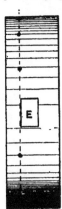

Fig. 131.—End View of Bowl.

polished. The fingerboard may be left plain or it may
have small pearl stars or discs inlaid, as a guide when
playing, or, if preferred, it can be fretted.

The bowl (see Figs. 129 and 131) may be of metal
nickel-plated, and is 6¾ in. or 7 in. in diameter by 2 in.
wide. The two edges are rolled or spun over as shown,
and the inside is fitted with a hard wood hoop, ₃⁄₁₆ in.
thick and about 1⅝ in. wide. A hole E (Fig. 131), 1 in.
by ⅝ in., is cut and filed a good fit to the handle, the
lower end of which is partly sunk into the wooden
hoop. A taper screw (Fig. 132), ₃⁄₁₆ in. diameter by 1 in.
long, clamps the handle firmly across the centre of the
bowl. If the nickel plated bowl cannot be procured, an

alternative method would be to get one of oak or beech,
which may be had, bent to shape and ready for gluing,
at almost any musical instrument maker's.

To hold the parchment, another hoop or ring is procured already plated, or, for the wooden bowl, may be
built up as follows : From a strip of brass, $\frac{1}{4}$ in. wide by
$\frac{1}{16}$ in. thick, bend the ring, as shown by F (Fig. 133), to
fit over the bowl, with about $\frac{1}{16}$ in. clearance all round.
The ends should be filed square across and brazed
together ; then clean off the ring and round it off quite
true. Another ring G, $\frac{1}{2}$ in. wide by $\frac{1}{16}$ in. thick, is then

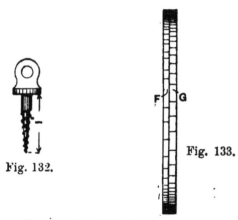

Fig. 132.

Fig. 133.

Fig. 132.—Taper Screw.   Fig. 133.—Section of Banjo Ring.

made, and should be a good fit over the smaller one.
Now with emery cloth brighten the inside of the larger
ring and the outside of the smaller ring, and tap one
within the other, as shown in Fig. 133, sweating them
together, and then cleaning, polishing, and lacquering
the whole. Now procure 2 ft. of $\frac{3}{16}$ in. brass wire (iron
is sometimes used, but is apt to rust and so spoil the
parchment), and bend it to form a ring that should be
just an easy fit over the bowl, allowance being made for
the thickness of parchment ; then braze the ends
together.

At $1\frac{7}{16}$in. from the top edge of the bowl twelve $\frac{3}{16}$-in.

clearing holes are drilled, as shown by Fig. 131, and hold
the clamping screws, one kind of which is shown by
Figs. 134 to 136. The hole H is $\frac{3}{16}$ in. diameter, and at
right angles to it another hole is drilled and tapped with

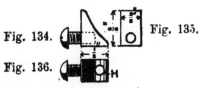

Fig. 134.   Fig. 135.

Fig. 136.

Figs.134-136.—Clamp and Screw.

a $\frac{3}{16}$ in. thread, to take a short round-headed screw and
washer, by which it is firmly fastened to the bowl from
the inside. Through the hole H the $\frac{3}{32}$-in. screw (Fig. 137),
2 in. long, passes.

Another screw (Fig. 138) of about the same size, and
having either a round or hexagon head, is required to
hold the tail-piece (Fig. 139). This piece may conveniently be made from brass, $\frac{3}{32}$ in. thick, 2½ in. wide,
by 1½ in., and five small holes are drilled through it at
the top to take the strings, one of which will come from
the peg A (Fig. 128) over a small round-headed screw J.

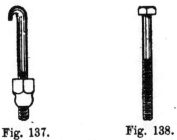

Fig. 137.   Fig. 138.

Fig. 137.—Clamping Screw for Parchment.
Fig. 138.—Clamping Screw for Tailpiece.

A $\frac{3}{16}$-in. hole is also drilled in the tail-piece for the screw
(Fig. 138), which also passes through the hole in Fig. 132
and is held by a nut from underneath.
·· Directions for putting on a parchment head have

already been given in this chapter. The kind of strings used is purely optional ; some players prefer gut, others wire. The bridge (Fig. 140) is 1¾ in. long by ⅟₁₆ in. deep, the taper section being ¼ in. thick at the bottom.

The banjo, being American in its origin, and peculiarly adapted to the musical temperament of our cousins across the water, possibly appeals even more to the Americans themselves than to English people. Consequently there is more thought and workmanship bestowed on its production in the United States than in this country ; and it may be observed that in some details the best American instruments still keep ahead

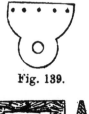

Fig. 139.

Fig. 140.

Fig. 139.—Tail-piece of Banjo. Fig. 140.—Bridge.

of those produced in England. The remainder of this chapter will deal with the head (or skin) of the banjo and the correct (American) method of putting it on. The method to be described is not generally known, and, in fact, has been regarded in America as a trade secret. In the ordinary method the head is put on, trimmed, and allowed to remain till gradually pulled down to compensate for the constant slackening. Finally the edge either splits from the edge of the rim or cannot be pulled down any farther, and is worthless. In the method about to be explained, a good head can be put on, and when set will remain hard and tight almost indefinitely, merely requiring half a turn of the screw hooks at long intervals when exposed to damp weather.

The American process begins in the same way as the

usual method. The first thing is to select a head. The best known make is stamped "J. Rogers Standard," and is used by the best English and American banjo makers. For an 11-in. banjo, a head not less than 14 in. in diameter should be chosen. Select as thick a head as can be found, because, when once put on properly, it remains harder and tighter than a thin one, especially in a damp climate ; furthermore, it seems to give off a far fuller and more powerful tone. It must be remembered that three-quarters of the tone of a banjo probably depends on the head. Choose a head of even thickness all over, which can be fairly accurately ascertained by feeling with fingers and thumb. In an uneven head the thicker parts will pull away from the thinner parts, and eventually cause a split. Most people prefer a head that is white all over, for the sake of appearance, but a partially white one is probably just as good for practical results.

It may here be said that the rim is the hoop or body of the banjo. The band or stretcher band is the metal band, about ½ in. deep, which fits over the rim and pulls down the head. The ring is of wire, which is enveloped by the head, and, being brought down over the top of the rim, is pressed down by the band. This ring must be of brass, and preferably nickel-plated, as when it is of iron or steel wire it invariably rusts and in time affects the skin, causing a split. The steel wire ring can be made less liable to rust by giving it several coats of spirit varnish, having previously polished the wire with emery paper.

Having removed the rim from the neck of the banjo, the old head must be taken off, and all the screw hooks taken out of the brackets. The new head must then be soaked in cold water, and in five or ten minutes will be sufficiently pliable to manipulate. Dry off all the surplus moisture with a towel, and place the head flat across the top of the rim so that its edge projects at an even distance from the rim all round. Next slip the wire ring over the head and top edge of the rim. In conjunction with the stretcher band, fold the surplus edge of the head back over the ring, turning up the edge the head over the ring and tucking it under the band, which has now been placed on top of the rim ready to receive it. A portion of the edge of the skin, say a few inches, should be tucked under the band at a time, till the whole has been got under all the way round. The band is then resting on the ring, which is wrapped round by the skin, and the edge of the skin is inside the band. The wire ring must be just far enough down the rim to hold. Now a screw hook may be put in a bracket and hooked on to the band to hold it in place ; another may be put on opposite, and a couple more at equal distances. They must not be screwed though, as the object is to keep the wire ring as near the top of the rim as possible. See that there are no wrinkles or creases in the part of the head that is round the wire ring. The head itself is, of course, in quite a slack state. Now the edge of the head may be pulled up with the fingers all round till the main surface is smooth and free from wrinkles, and another screw or two may be added to help in keeping the band in position, extra long screws being necessary for the preliminary process. Having the head as tight as possible with the fingers—pulling evenly all round the edge of the skin, and pressing on the band with the other hand—it may be still further pulled with a pair of broad-nosed pliers. Then more long screws can be added up to a dozen or so, but always bear in mind that the band must not yet be pulled down ; in fact, the band at this stage must not be much more than, say, $\frac{1}{8}$ in. down the rim. If the head has been cleverly managed it will now be quite smooth, though, of course, slack and limp owing to its dampness.

Now put the rim with the head into a dry, but not hot, place, and there let it remain till the head seems dry and hard. This will probably take two or three hours. It should then appear very fairly tight, but must be smooth and even. Now comes a point which is not in general use, and to which particular attention is drawn. Take off the long screw hooks and remove the stretcher band. Next slip the head off the rim with its wire ring in it. Place the head in a warm room, such as a kitchen, though not near a fire, and rest it or hang it in such a position that the air circulates freely all around it, and let it remain all night. Next day it will be noticed that the head has become quite flat, though the ring remains tightly enfolded round it. The slight shoulder which has been produced all around it by over-lapping the rim, and by being pressed down within the band, will have almost or entirely disappeared. The reason is as follows : The head, having been in a soaked condition, the face—that is, the main part of it—will have become dry when on the rim, while the part under the stretcher band and ring remains damp. If the head had been left in this state on the rim, that part of the head would never have dried out like the main part, and on screwing down the head only the damp portion under the band would have been stretched. This would become thinner with constant stretching, till in time it would break. Now, by the process which has been explained, of removing the head and allowing it to dry throughout, the head is fixed round the wire ring without any damp parts to be taken into consideration. Next carefully clean off with chamois leather the upper part of the rim over which the head will be pulled down, and slightly grease the edge and upper part of the rim with the best vaseline, which will have no deleterious effect whatever on the skin, while the slight lubrication will enable the head to be pulled down without much friction against the rim.

Having placed the head on the rim, take the stretcher band and fit it over the part of the head round the wire ring. It will not clutch the rim yet, as the head is quite hard and flat, and will almost have to be balanced on top. Then fit six or eight long screws, meanwhile trying to keep the band in proper position. On slightly screwing down the hooks, it will be found that the head comes down quite easily, and gets a grip over the rim. Now add more long hooks, and pull it down till the short hooks which belong to the banjo will just reach. These can be substituted one by one for the long ones till the full complement of hooks is in position. During this operation the greatest care must be taken to pull the head evenly all around, and this must be constantly gauged with a rule or piece of wood from the bottom edge of the rim. As long as the wire ring and bottom edge of the banjo are parallel, the head will be evenly stretched, providing the banjo is accurately made and the rim is not warped. When the head is pulled quite tight, let the stretcher band stand a good half of its depth above the rim for half a day or more, and then give another turn or two to the screw hooks. The head might be pulled down now till the band is sufficiently low to allow the strings to come clear of it after the neck has been replaced, but it is far better to pull the head gradually to the proper level, even if two or three days are taken to do it. When the band has been pulled down about two-thirds of its depth, the surplus edge of the skin may be trimmed off. This requires care, and the least touch of the knife blade on the strained skin may ruin all the work. A safe and easy way to do it is to take a flat piece of tin, about 4 in. square, and with the shears shape one side to fit inside the band. Hold the tin firmly on the head and press close against the inside of the band. The surface of the head is thus entirely protected, and a knife with a very sharp point may be used to cut off the surplus skin. By driving the point right through the part to be cut to the band itself, it can be easily worked along. When a length of nearly 4 in. has been cut, the tin must be slid farther along, and so on, till the whole of the surface has been trimmed off. The blade of the knife should be kept level with the surface of the tin.

So that the banjo may be used before the band has got down to its proper level, it is an excellent plan to file down a part of the band equal to the width of the neck, where the finger-board joins the rim. . The portion filed out should be about $\frac{1}{8}$ in. to $\frac{3}{16}$ in. in depth, and should then be level with the head at the juncture of the fingerboard and rim. This will leave $\frac{1}{8}$ in. to $\frac{3}{16}$ in. of the rest of the band standing above the head, and this is the right height. In time to come occasional pulling will bring the band down to the level of the head, though it will be a long time hence if well put on. There may be a little difficulty with the tail-piece, owing to the band standing high ; however, there are various adjustable tail-pieces in the market which overcome this.

Another matter which might have been alluded to earlier is the side of the head to be used on top. One side of each head is found to be quite smooth, and the other much rougher. The latter is the flesh side, and being the softer side of the two has greater stretching power. Therefore it should be uppermost. The head should always be tight, and so hard that it is difficult to make an impression on it when bearing down hard with the finger ; also the bridge, when up, should not make any perceptible impression on the head.

A banjo should always be kept in a thoroughly dry place and in a case or green baize bag, and should not be exposed to draughts more than can be helped. The head is as sensitive as a barometer, but, nevertheless, when well put on it will remain in perfect condition with ordinary care and only require pulling down at rare intervals. It is an excellent plan to fit two heads on, thus having a spare one ready fitted, with its ring, and occasionally take the head off the banjo and give it a rest for a month or two in a dry place, replacing it with the spare head. By doing this the head is "rested," and the result in both tone and wearing qualities will be most gratifying. It also saves much trouble to have an already fitted head to put on at once in the event of one breaking.

The greater the diameter of a banjo the more surface of skin is exposed to the atmosphere, and in the British damp climate that must be always reckoned with. Even in America all modern banjos are now made with rims only 10 in. to 11 in. across. Till recently concert banjos were generally 12 in. to 13 in. in diameter, but it is now found that by diminishing the area of head, and proportionately increasing the length of the neck, a sharper and more ringing tone is obtained, and there is less susceptibility to weather conditions. It was a fallacy to suppose that the larger the head the greater the volume of tone.

It is as well to mention that the above description of putting on a head applies only to the American pattern of banjo, and not to the zither banjo. To obtain the quality of tone of the zither banjo, the Americans use in preference the autoharp, which sounds better and is learnt and played with much greater ease, while it possesses greater capabilities of full harmonies and power.

In the event of a head splitting on a banjo, it is necessary to cut it all along the edge with a sharp knife at once, supposing it is not convenient at the moment to remove it and replace it with a new one. When the head is split, the strain at once becomes uneven, and if left in position any length of time the rim will be pulled entirely out of shape.

CHAPTER X.

ZITHER MAKING.

ZITHERS are known in a variety of shapes, but the principal two are the Élégie zither, alto zither, or song zither (Fig. 141), and the concert zither (Fig. 142), known also as the prim zither, horn zither, or Schlag zither. The last term is applied because it is struck in a manner

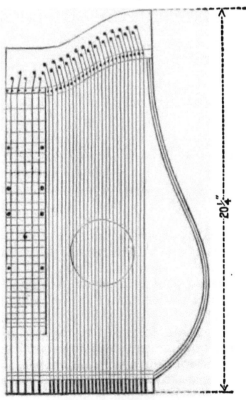

Fig. 141.—Élégie Zither.

quite different from that of the Streich zither, this
being the alpine violin or bow zither, which will be
found illustrated by Fig. 155 on p. 135. It is venturing
on disputed ground to say anything as to the relative
merits of the Élégie and concert zithers, but the former
is generally recognised as the correct instrument for song
accompaniments and sentimental solos, being claimed by
some to have a much sounder tone and longer vibrations.
On the other hand, the concert zither is considered the
most serviceable for general use, its shape is much more

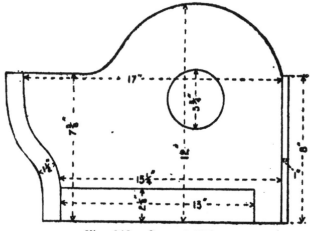

Fig. 142.—Concert Zither.

graceful, and it offers more resistance to the very great
stress of the strings. The concert zither is the one in
use among the peasantry of the Tyrol.

The practical information about to be given is on the
construction of the instrument shown by Fig. 141, but
is also applicable to that shown by Fig. 142. With
regard to materials, there will be required 2 ft. of the
best Swiss pine, $\frac{3}{16}$ in. by 12 in., for the back (Swiss pine,
under the name of belly wood, can be obtained from any
timber merchant who supplies pianoforte makers) ; a
piece of mahogany, rosewood, or another piece of pine of
the same thickness for the belly ; a strip of maple or

sycamore, $\frac{3}{16}$ in. by $\frac{7}{8}$ in., and 24 in. long, for the ribs
on the curved side; another piece of the same for the
straight side, 19 in. long; a piece of pine for the stays,
15 in. long by $\frac{3}{4}$ in., and about 3 in. wide; a piece of
beech for the blocks, 10 in. long, $\frac{3}{4}$ in. thick, and 5 in.

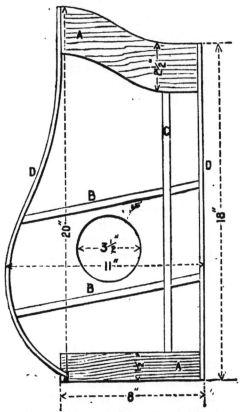

Fig. 143.—Under Side of Zither Belly.

wide; a piece of ebony, 13 in. long, $\frac{3}{16}$ in. thick, and $2\frac{1}{4}$
in. wide, for the fingerboard; another piece of the same,
7 in. long and 1 in. wide, from which to get out the
upper bridge; a piece of ebony or rosewood, $\frac{3}{8}$ in. thick,
1 in. wide, and $8\frac{1}{2}$ in. long, for the lower bridge; and a
small piece from which to make three knobs for feet.

All the thicknesses here given, with the exception of the stuff for the stays, are for finished material as it will be required.; but lengths and widths are given a little more than wanted, to allow for working. In addition to the stuff necessary for the instrument itself, there will be required a piece on which to build, unless the bench-top is preferred for the purpose. This piece must be 24 in. in length, 18 in. wide, and any thickness not less than ¾ in.; it must be planed true on one side. A piece of wood ¾ in. by 6 in. wide, and 24 in. long, will be required for a mould for the curved side; and a few more odd pieces of ½-in. stuff will be necessary.

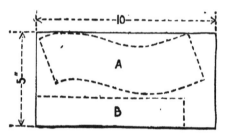

Fig. 144.—Getting Out Top and Bottom Blocks.

Begin the construction of the zither by getting out a stiff paper pattern to the shape of Fig. 141. Cut off ¼ in. from the bottom edge; then turn it over, and on the reverse side mark the position of all blocks A, stays B and C, and the sound-hole as in Fig. 143; cut out the sound-hole, and the pattern is ready. Now take the pieces intended for back and belly, which have been reduced to the thickness previously given, and mark on them the outline of the pattern; cut these out, and shape them up exactly alike, leaving the edges perfectly square. Lay the back on one side, and, taking the belly, lay it face down-wards on the slab or bench, and fasten it there with two screws, through the place where the sound-hole will be. Put these screws through another piece of wood, about ½ in. thick and 2 in. wide first, as the belly itself is not strong enough. Now take the piece of beech 5 in. by 10 in. by ¾ in., lay upon it the pattern, and mark along the top, then shift it 2½ in. lower, and mark again ; then mark off $\frac{3}{16}$ in. from each end, and this will give the pattern for the wrest-pin block A (Fig. 144). From the remaining piece can be got the lower block, 1½ in. by 8 in. (see B Fig. 144). Square the edges of these, and lay the upper block in its place at the top of the belly, flush with the top edge, and leaving $\frac{3}{16}$ in. at each end for the ribs to come on. Now lay the lower block in its place, and mark where the end of the curved rib will come ; then cut a piece ½ in. deep and $\frac{3}{16}$ in. wide out of the end of the block, for the end of the rib to fit into, as shown in Fig. 143. This block is now ready, and both it and the top one may be glued into their places, and weighted down till dry. When doing this, take care

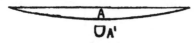

Fig. 145.—Diagonal Stay.

that the $\frac{3}{16}$ in. of the belly is left at each end of the upper block, but at the straight end only of the lower block. In gluing on the blocks, have them well warmed, and take care that the glue is quite hot, clean, and strong, but not thick.

While the blocks are drying, get out the two diagonal stays, the shape of which is shown in Fig. 145, where A indicates a section through the centre of a stay. These stays taper off to nothing at each end, and go quite across the belly, the lower one starting from a point 5½ in., and the upper one 10½ in., from the bottom on the straight side, and being carried across to points, 2½ in. lower, on the opposite side. They should be ½ in. deep in the centre, and ½ in. wide throughout. They may be glued on, and cramped down by a button at each end, and by means of a piece that is already holding the belly down to the

board ; for this purpose take off the piece, alter its
position as may be necessary, and re-fasten with longer
screws (see A, Fig. 146).

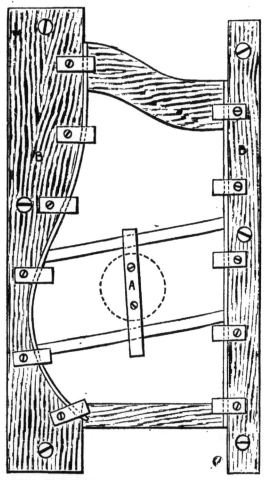

Fig. 146.—Zither in Mould and Cramps.

For the ribs D (Fig. 143) an outside mould is required. On the piece of wood, 6 in. wide, 24 in. long,
and ¾ in. thick, lay the curved side of the pattern, and
mark along its edge ; then cut it out, and clean up the

hollow side, and, taking up the buttons from the ends of
the stays, screw this down side by side with, and exactly
fitting, the curved side of the belly. The remaining
piece can be screwed down at the straight side, and the
belly will then be in a mould B (Fig. 146). On the top
of these pieces screw wood buttons, about 2 in. long and
1 in. wide, at intervals of 3 in., and the arrangement is
complete. Before gluing in the ribs, it is as well to see
that everything fits properly. Take the slip prepared
for the ribs, and reduce it to ¾ in. wide ; insert one end
of it in the groove in the lower block, and gently bend it
round the curved side, screwing the buttons down on to it
as the work proceeds. If the wood is harsh or brittle,
it will be as well to damp it before doing this. Mark
the places where the ends of the diagonal stays come ;
take the slip out again, and cut out the little pieces
that may be necessary ; then replace it, and fit accurately.

Fig. 147.—Long Stay.

The straight side must be fitted in the same manner ;
and when this is done the ribs may be glued in and
cramped down, and the whole left to dry (see Fig. 146).
The interior construction is now nearly complete,
requiring only the addition of the long stay or inner
bridge C (Fig. 143), shown separately by Fig. 147. This
is 13½ in. long, ¾ in. deep, and ⅝ in. thick, and must fit
tightly between the top and bottom blocks. Two curved
pieces are cut out of the under edge to give lightness to
it, and two square pieces out of the upper edge to receive
the diagonal stays ; and if the blocks are thoroughly dry
this long stay may be glued into its place. After
another interval for drying, the cramps may all be taken
off, the shell taken out of the mould, and the sound-hole
cut. This is 3½ in. in diameter, and must have its edges
neatly rounded. A straightedge must now be passed
over the blocks, ribs, and stay, to see that all are exactly
level, and any inequality must be rectified.

When all is ready the back may be prepared for fixing. Glue a small block, 1 in. square and ¼ in. thick, at the widest part of the inside of the back, ₁³₆ in. from the edge ; this is to take the stem of a foot that will afterwards be fastened in.   Mark on the outside of the back where the centre of this block comes.   Now replace the shell in the mould, and refix the buttons in their places, turning them to one side to leave the top edges of the ribs bare.   All being ready, and the glue

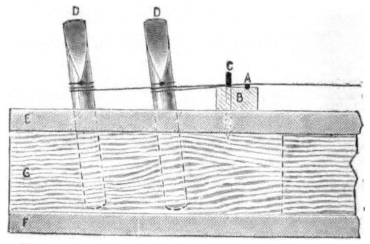

Fig. 148.—Upper Block and Bridge, with Wrest-pins, etc.

quite hot, pass a warm flat-iron several times over the blocks to get them warm ; then glue quickly all the points of contact with the back, namely, the blocks, the edges of the ribs, and the feet of the long stay ; and, as soon as this is done, put on the back, and weigh down at top and bottom ; turn the buttons into their places, and screw down.   It being absolutely necessary that the contact with all the points should be perfect, it is better not to attempt it without assistance.   When all is quite dry the instrument may be taken out of the mould, the edges cleaned up, and, with the back and belly, thoroughly smoothed with glass-paper.

Now prepare the bridges and fingerboard.   First cut

out the upper bridge from the piece of ebony, 1 in. wide and 7 in. long ; when finished this will be ⅜ in. wide and ₁₆ in. thick, and will have a small groove cut in at a distance of ⅛ in. from the front edge, to take a piece of No. 18 brass wire, over which the strings are to pass. This is the pressure-bar A (Fig. 148). Glue bridge B on with its bottom edge 2½ in. from the top edge of the wrest-pin block, and its left end 2⅛ in. from the straight side ; the remaining distance to the edge will be occupied by the fingerboard. (In Fig. 148, c

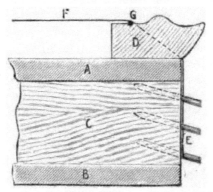

Fig. 149.—Section of Lower End or Zither.

indicates the bridge-pins, D the wrest-pins, E the belly, F the back, and G the block.)

The lower bridge may now be got out of the piece of ebony or rosewood, 1 in. by ⅜ in. by 8½ in. ; and this, when finished, should be of the exact size and pattern of D (Fig. 149), and the exact length of the straight part at the bottom of the instrument.

The strings do not pass completely over the lower bridge, but partly over and partly through it—over it as far as the pressure-bar, and then through channels to where the bridge joins the top edge of the belly. The first five channels are cut at intervals of ⅜ in. from each other, leaving ₁₆ in. of the fingerboard on the outside of the first and fifth strings respectively ; then allow a further interval of ⅛ in., and divide the remainder of

the bridge, leaving $\frac{1}{4}$ in. at the bass end, into twenty-six
equal parts. These marks, which will be about $\frac{7}{32}$ in.
apart, must be sawn through diagonally (as shown in
Fig. 149) from the pressure-bar to the belly, and the
lower of the channels thus made must be wider than
the others, as the strings going through them will be
thicker. It is better, perhaps, to glue the bridge on
(leaving $\frac{1}{4}$ in. projecting over the end), and let it dry
before cutting through it, as it is less liable to fracture
then. In Fig. 149 A indicates the belly, B the back, C
the block, D the lower bridge, E the hitch-pins, F the
strings, and G the pressure-bar.

The finger- or fretboard, when finished, should be
13 in. long, $2\frac{1}{8}$ in. wide, and $\frac{3}{16}$ in. thick. At a distance
of $\frac{1}{4}$ in. from the top draw a line across, and on this line
cut a groove $\frac{3}{32}$ in. deep—that is, exactly half-way
through the board. In this groove insert a piece of
sheet brass or German silver, which must project $\frac{1}{8}$ in.
above the top surface. This forms the nut, and from
the front edge of this all the distances for the other
frets are measured. Directly at the back of this nut
five holes are drilled, sloping to the left, in which to
insert the nut pins. These holes correspond to the five
channels in the lower bridge, in being $\frac{3}{8}$ in. from each
other. Now proceed to mark off the fingerboard for
the frets, the distances given on p. 127 being from the
front edge of the nut to the centre of each fret, so that
the mark must in each case be cut out.

When all are marked, proceed to cut carefully each
one to a depth of $\frac{3}{32}$ in., except Nos. 23 and 25, which are
short frets, and go only half-way across the board. For
this purpose a very fine dovetail saw must be used.
Having cut all the grooves, fill in each one with a piece
of brass or German silver, allowing $\frac{1}{16}$ in. only to remain
above the surface.

To fasten the frets in their places securely, take a
small quantity of shellac, crush it to powder, and place
a little in each groove, then heat the fret by holding it
in a flame, and place it quickly in position. Note: do

DISTANCES FOR FRETS ON FINGERBOARD.

1st.—$\frac{7}{8}$ in.	16th.—$9\frac{3}{16}$ in.
2nd.—$1\frac{11}{16}$ in.	17th.—$9\frac{9}{16}$ in.
3rd.—$2\frac{7}{16}$ in.	18th.—$9\frac{7}{8}$ in.
4th.—$3\frac{3}{16}$ in.	19th.—$10\frac{1}{16}$ in.
5th.—$3\frac{13}{16}$ in.	20th.—$10\frac{3}{8}$ in.
6th.—$4\frac{7}{16}$ in.	21st.—$10\frac{3}{4}$ in.
7th.—$5\frac{1}{16}$ in.	22nd.—11 in.
8th.—$5\frac{5}{8}$ in.	23rd.—$11\frac{1}{4}$ in.
9th.—$6\frac{3}{16}$ in.	24th.—$11\frac{1}{2}$ in.
10th.—$6\frac{11}{16}$ in.	25th.—$11\frac{11}{16}$ in.
11th.—$7\frac{3}{16}$ in.	26th.—$11\frac{7}{8}$ in.
12th.—$7\frac{5}{8}$ in.	27th.—$12\frac{1}{16}$ in.
13th.—$8\frac{1}{16}$ in.	28th.—$12\frac{1}{4}$ in.
14th.—$8\frac{1}{2}$ in.	29th.—$12\frac{7}{16}$ in.
15th.—$8\frac{7}{8}$ in.	

not make it red-hot, or it will burn the shellac instead of melting it. The rough edges and ends of the frets must be rounded off, and the dots or stops may be inserted. These are of ivory or pearl, $\frac{3}{16}$ in. in diameter. Two are inserted half-way between the fourth and fifth, the eighth and ninth, the eleventh and twelfth, and the eighteenth and nineteenth frets; one on each side of the board; and one between the fourteenth and fifteenth, in the centre. These dots are guides to fingering (see Fig. 141, p. 117).

The board may now be placed in position. First, warm it well; then glue it over, and quickly lay it in its place, giving it a rub up and down to set the glue, and taking care that the nut is level with the groove in the upper bridge, and the outer edge flush with the straight side. Clean off the glue that has squeezed out, and set aside for a few hours to dry. The whole may now be thoroughly cleaned up, and the holes bored in the back for the insertion of the feet, one at the top and one at the bottom of the straight side, and one at the widest part of the curved side, where there is a block ready for it.

These feet are small round knobs, ½ in. in diameter, with a stem ¼ in., and when in position have a sharp little iron spike projecting from the bottom, to prevent the instrument slipping about on the table when being played.

The back and ribs may now be stained and the instrument polished, unless it is to be purfled. For this purpose about 4 ft. of purfling will be required; this is sufficient to go round the curved side and the sound-hole. It may be said that varnish does not give very satisfactory results; the instrument should be French-polished, as this admits of a very much better finish, especially if the belly is of maple or rosewood. Varnish, especially spirit varnish, shows every little scratch or chip, and soon wears rough; and because of its drying so quickly when applied it is difficult to get a good finish when it is spread over a flat surface.

When polished, the wrest-pin block may be bored. First, bore the holes for the melody string. A reference to Fig. 141 (p. 117) will show where these are to be, and care must be taken that they are a little to the right of the holes for the nut pins. The pins for the accompaniment strings occupy the centre portion of the block, are $\frac{7}{16}$ in. apart, and are placed in two rows, ¾ in. apart, the pins of one row alternating with those of the other, and the whole sloping slightly to the top of the block. After boring they should be slightly countersunk. The bridge-pins of the accompaniment strings are $\frac{7}{32}$ in. apart, and slope to the right. All these bridge-pins should be made of No. 20 brass wire, and be ¾ in. in length, with ⅛ in. left above the bridge. The holes for them should be drilled, not bored. The wrest-pins are of a special kind, and can be bought for a small sum. They can be had either in blue steel, polished steel, or nickelled, the latter being preferable.

The work now remaining is the insertion of the hitch-pins, shown at E (Fig. 149, p. 125). The lower row consists of the first five strings only, and are put in a straight line; the two other rows alternate with each other, and the whole corresponds to the thirty-one channels through the lower bridge. These pins are made of No. 17 wire, are ¼ in. long, and are driven into the block for ½ in. Now fit a piece of the No. 17 wire into the groove in each bridge, and the instrument is ready for stringing.

The two methods of stringing zithers most in vogue are known respectively as the Stuttgart and Vienna methods. Fig. 150 represents the open notes of the melody strings (the five strings on the finger-board) of a zither strung on the Stuttgart system, while Fig. 151 shows the Vienna method, which is the one most general. Silk and gut strings are not only worthless as to tone, but it is hopeless to attempt to keep them in tune. Procure good metallic strings, which are to be had in sets contained in boxes. Such sets of strings should not cost more than from 4s. to 7s. 6d. complete, and a good set will last three years unless the player's hands are of a very moist nature, when, of course, the strings gradually rust under the wrapping, and the tone suffers, not the string. The sets mentioned may not, perhaps, include the steel and brass wire for the three first melody strings, but the fourth and fifth—that is, G and C—both metal covered with metal, are included. Each separate string has its number and note on a label, and possibly the set may contain more strings than there is accommodation for. This is because a zither may have any number of strings, from twenty-two to thirty-two Simply start at E flat (having first strung the finger-board), no matter whether numbered one or two. Some sets give G sharp as the first of the accompaniment strings, but disregard it. As for any there may be over, simply discard them; they are not required for their legitimate place, but come in useful when the player chances to break a string of similar calibre or gauge—an event which need never happen if care is taken to strain each string slowly and carefully, using frequent friction along its length in the process.

All idea of purchasing zither strings by gauge should be dismissed; this might answer for the dulcimer or

I

pianoforte, but every string for zither use is made specially
for the note it is intended to give when stretched to a
certain tension ; hence there are hardly any two alike.
For this reason the accompaniment and bass strings,
that is, all beyond the five on the. finger-board, are
always sold in sets, each string having a loop made in
one end for affixing to the pins of the tail-piece.

Do not string right up all at once, as many strings are
caused to break in this way. Make it a two days' job,
and strain well before finally fetching up to pitch.
Never go higher than half a tone lower than piano pitch,

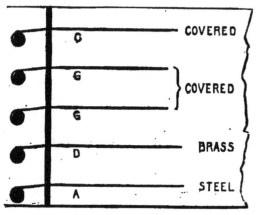

Fig. 150.—Stuttgart Method of Tuning Zither.

unless it is wished to accompany another instrument,
which zither players are, as a rule, not fond of, except in
the case of such instruments as the guitar or mandoline,
which can always be made to accord with the more
delicate zither. Having obtained the strings, including
a reel of special steel and brass wire, cut off a piece of steel
wire longer by 3 in. or 4 in. than the length of the instrument from tail-piece to pegs. This is to form one of the
three melody strings. Then, with suitable pliers or with
the fingers, form a very small loop at one end, the smaller
the better. Pass this loop over the pin at the tail-piece
end and the string up through the groove in the latter.

Then run the string through the finger and thumb of
the right hand, so as to have it perfectly straight and
free from "kinks." Insert not more than 1 in. through
the peg-hole, and, with the tuning-key, wind the string
evenly on the peg, using the right elbow to keep the
looped end from springing out of the groove, or off the
pin, and the right hand to guide the string evenly on the
peg. When the string just "bites," and there is no fear
of its springing out of place, leave it and pass on to the
next, taking care in each case to pass the top of the
string behind the little pin behind the nut (see Fig. 141,

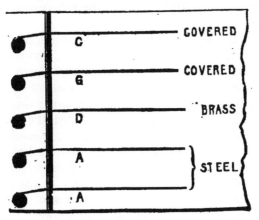

Fig. 151.—Viennese Method of Tuning Zither.

p. 117). When the three wire strings are on, the work
becomes simpler because all the others are already provided with proper loops, which only want looping on to
the pins and through the groove. However, take pre-
cautions against twisting and "kinking." Also be very
careful in unwrapping each string, as any actual bend in
a string would probably result in a break.

A further word on the choice of strings may now be
said. Zither players are divided on the question as to
which are better, wire or silk and gut. Wire strings
have been recommended here owing to their tone and
ability to stand in tune, but it is only fair to state that

many players would use these only on the fret-board ;
the great tension of wire strings, they claim, ruins the
grip of the tuning pegs, and with it the instrument, and
the tone yielded is harsh and clanging. On the other
hand, the opponents of silk and gut strings say that only
in the hands of inferior players are the wire strings
harsh ; that they make for greater delicacy of touch, and
that they do not destroy the grip of the pegs, instancing
in support of the last statement the method of stringing
a piano. Furthermore, say the exponents of the wire
strings, these are accurately balanced as to tension,
whereas it is scarcely possible to get two gut or silk
strings alike.

The tuning of the zither is carried out in the following
manner : Having got all the strings on, proceed to raise
them carefully, beginning at the first. Fetch that one
up to about E (under the stave) by the aid of a pianoforte
or tuning-fork. Treat the next similarly ; this also has,
eventually, to come up to A. Fetch the brass wire
string up to about B, and so on, straining carefully each
string. Now leave the strings to stretch all night, after
which proceed to tune the second string to A, then the
first to it. Then place the forefinger of the left hand
behind the fifth fret (where the first spot is) and tune
the brass string to it, but an octave lower. Then stop
the D string on the fifth fret, and tune the G to it, and
the same with the next, which is C. Then the
finger-board is complete, and in tune. Now tune the
accompaniment strings, which comprise the first twelve
after those on the finger-board. Tune these according
to the table shown on p. 133.

The thirteenth string is tuned an octave lower than
the first, the fourteenth an octave lower than the second,
and so on throughout. Some strings in the bass, which
begins at the thirteenth, are usually tuned two octaves
lower—such are C and D—but these are easily recognised
by their greater thickness, and the utter impossibility
of getting them up another octave.

The systems of stringing and tuning have by no means

Number of String.	Name of Note.	How to form it for tuning.
1	D sharp	On the first fret of the D string.
2	B flat	„ third „ G „
3	F	„ „ „ D „
4	C	„ fifth „ G „
5	G	„ „ „ D „
6	D	By the open D string.
7	A	On the second fret of the G string.
8	E	„ „ „ D „
9	B	„ fourth „ G „
10	F sharp	„ „ „ D „
11	C sharp	„ sixth „ G „
12	G sharp	„ „ „ D „

escaped controversy. For instance, some players hold that Fig. 150, p. 130, does not show the real Stuttgart method, and that Fig. 151 illustrates the Munich rather than the Viennese system. The following is a brief statement of their case :—The Stuttgart school has two methods ; these are C, G, D, A, E, E from below up, entailing a sixth string, or C, G, D, A, A, E, E composed of seven strings :

The true Viennese stringing is C, G, G, D, A, which, to be correct, must have the G between the G and D tuned one octave above the other. The Munich method is the only correct one harmonically, and is C, G, D, A, A, the two A's being tuned alike, the others being each one-fifth above one another. All the other strings of the zither are tuned in fifths, and as already stated.

Anyone intending to make a zither would find it worth while to adopt the shape shown by Fig. 152. It is known as the Arion, and was designed by a well-known specialist some years ago. It embodies several distinct improvements over the usual type, foremost among which are the greater area of the "tables," or sound-boards, which, of course, admits of a far greater volume of sound, not, however, at the expense of any of the pure, distinctive tones peculiar to the zither. Then, again, the strings are affixed by means of pins, as in the guitar, this enhancing the appearance, and the attachment of the tail-piece to the belly is by some supposed to improve the tone also. The Arion is played in the same way as the ordinary zither, and anyone capable of building a

Fig. 152.—Arion Zither.   Fig. 153.—Harp Zither.

zither of the usual shape would have no great difficulties to contend with in the construction of the Arion.

Allied to the Arion is the harp zither (two forms of which are illustrated by Figs. 153 and 154). This form of the zither was originally designed to accommodate a large number of supplementary bass and contra-bass strings, but such additional strings are of very limited use ; still, the extremely elegant design might be followed to advantage, especially as it presents no insuperable obstacles to the constructor.

Zither instruments of the viol class are shown by

Figs. 155 and 156, the former being the Streich or bow zither or alpine violin, and the latter the philomela or

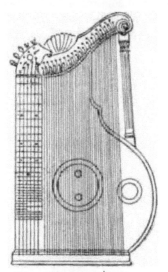

Fig. 154.—Harp Zither.

philomèle. Upon both elaborate violin music may be performed with proportionately little practice. Of the two, the earlier form is the Streich zither, this consisting of an upper and lower "table" or sound-board, of the

Fig. 155.—Streich or Bow Zither.

bellows-like form shown, the upper one being perforated with "rosettes," or sound-holes, of arbitrary shape. Along

the centre, or the greater portion of the length, runs a
slightly rounded fret-board, full instructions for the division of which into semitones have already been given in
these articles. Four metal strings are used, attached at
the " bridge " end, as on the zither proper, and strained

Fig. 156.—Philomela Zither, or Zither-viola.

by pegs in the ordinary way. The lowest is of steel
wire, wire-covered, and is tuned to G ; the second, also
covered wire, is tuned to D ; the third is a brass wire
tuned to A ; while the fourth is a fine steel wire tuned to
E. Thus the pitch, tuning, and compass of the instrument
are identical with those of the violin. Great facility of

execution may readily be acquired, as all the notes are formed by the frets ; while the bowing is done across the narrow end, which projects over the edge of the table for the purpose. A single leg, with a minute spike, is provided at about 2 in. from the tail-piece, while two others, somewhat higher, are placed one on each side of the wider part, as shown in Fig. 155. The tone of the bow zither is almost exactly the same as that of the violin, but is, unfortunately, rather thin and weak.

The philomela, or zither-viola, has been invented for the reason just given. This instrument approaches very nearly to the violin in tone and volume, and may be regarded as the perfect form of the Streich zither. Although it differs very much in shape, and is played in a different manner, there is no easier instrument of the viol type. The neck differs from that of any other instrument, inasmuch as it is square and of equal thickness through its whole length. It may be slightly rounded on the fret-board, and the divisions of the latter are the same as on any other form of zither. At the back of the "nut," or thereabouts, is a short spiked leg, which rests upon the edge of the table in playing, while the broad tail-piece end is supported upon the lap of the player. A somewhat shorter bow than usual is employed ; and, of course, the fingering is done with the thumb and first three fingers of the left hand. The latter is not curled round the neck as when holding the violin, but is held in a dropping position over the fret-board. The construction of the philomela offers no difficulties, as the back and belly may be left flat ; though, if curved as in the case of the violin, the instrument is much more shapely. The making of the rib is really the only delicate matter in making a philomela. As to the size, the viola, or tenor violin, may be taken as about correct; but, of course, the neck is wider. Sound-posts are employed, as in the violin. Machine heads are usually affixed.

A small and toy-like form of zither is known as the Prince of Wales' Harp (see Fig. 157). It is very easily

made, and consists simply of a shallow box, having at
top and bottom blocks of hard wood for the insertion of
the tuning or wrest pins, and the hitch pins, which are
placed in the outside edges, not in front. At the sides
are placed stout pieces of wood, and on these and the
blocks the sound-board is fixed. The top block slopes
at an angle of 45°. The strings pass over bridges
having on top stout brass wire to take the pressure.
The number of strings varies from eight to nineteen or

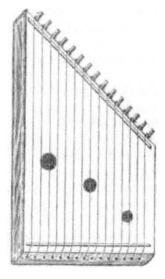

Fig. 157—Prince of Wales' Harp.

more, and the size of the instrument and length and
size of strings depend entirely upon the pitch required.
The instrument, even considered as a toy, is capable
of producing very sweet sounds, and is quite worth
the trouble of stringing up properly. To do this, the
following steel wire should be used : first and second
strings (beginning from the bottom, or longest), No. 12 ;
third and fourth, No. 11 ; fifth and sixth, No. 10;
seventh and eighth, No. 9 ; ninth and tenth, No. 8 ;
eleventh and twelfth, No. 7. If the first of these are

rather "twangy," it will be as well to substitute covered strings (copper on steel), such as are used for the fourth and fifth of the zither proper. The tuning is a very easy matter, the scale being the ordinary "diatonic" scale ; and it, of course, limits the tunes capable of being played on it to those standing within its compass, and containing no accidentals, either sharp or flat. If the instrument is not strengthened with stays, lengthwise, the considerable strain may not unlikely cause it to assume a very ungraceful curve, and drop out of tune as fast as it can be tightened up. Dulcimer pins are the most suitable for the purpose.

A sounding table for a zither may be made to any design to match other furniture or fit recesses, and the legs may be formed of any hard wood, but the top must be of good sound pine, about $\frac{3}{8}$ in. thick, nicely ebonised and polished, or of sequoia wood, finished in natural colour (or stained) and polished. A very good plan is to make the top of the table in the form of a hollow box, deep enough to store the instrument when not in use. If fitted with a lock, great care must be taken to prevent any "jar" on account of loose fitting in either lock or hinges.

The zither, when not in use, should be kept in a case. Either $\frac{1}{4}$-in. pine or American whitewood is suitable for a light case. It should be rectangular, the inside being shaped to fit the zither with strips of stout millboard or thin wood bent to shape. The remaining space may be fitted with partitions having lids, which will be found useful for containing tuning key, spare strings, etc. The outside may be covered with thin leather, or stained and polished to suit particular taste.

The plectrum used by zither players for "plucking" the strings is in the form of a ring, and this, to fit properly, should spring on over the thumbnail. Make one of horn, tortoiseshell, or metal, whichever is preferred. The former two give a better tone, being flexible. If horn is used, file up the prong, and then boil it to soften it, and bend it to fit while flexible.

If metal, then thick copper wire, filed to shape,'does very well. The proper shape is shown in Figs. 158 to 160, Fig. 158 representing the tongue before bending to shape,

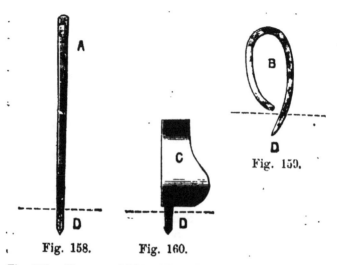

Fig. 158.   Fig. 160.

Fig. 159.

Fig. 158.—Tongue of Material to form Plectrum.   Fig. 159. —Ring, or Plectrum.   Fig. 160.—Concert Ring, or Plectrum.

Fig. 159 the ring after bending, and Fig. 160 the "concert ring." The only important part is the actual tongue D.

CHAPTER XI.

DULCIMER MAKING.

DULCIMERS may be made of almost any size provided the proportions are maintained, and although the instructions given in this chapter will relate more especially to the building of a "G" instrument, they will be equally applicable to any instrument, the only difference being in the relative dimensions of the various parts.

The tools required in the construction of the dulcimer are a hand saw, a small plane, a common brace, two gimlets (the smaller gimlet barely ⅛ in., the larger one barely ₁³₆ in.), a sprig bit, a hand hammer, a wood chisel (barely ¼ in. wide, to cut the groove for the sound-board), a screwdriver, a pair of cutting pliers, a small file, and a small paint brush.

The wood used should be thoroughly dry and seasoned, and free from all knots, blemishes, and shakes. For this reason entirely new wood is always preferable. The quantities required will be :—A piece of beech or oak (of the kind known as "pipe-stave"), 18 in. long and 3 in. by 3½ in. thick, for wrest-pin and hitch-pin blocks ; 6 ft. of 9 in. by ⅜ in. red deal, for the back ; 2 ft. 6 in. of 15 in. by ₁³₆ in., for the belly or sound-board ; this latter to be best pine, sequoia, or cedar. It is better to have this in one piece, so as to avoid, if possible, a joint in the board. If the necessary width cannot be obtained, and a joint is unavoidable, it should be secured at the back with buttons ¾ in. square by ₁³₆ in. thick, placed across the joint corner wise, and, when dry, the edges pared down to nothing.

The back and front braces, inside bridges, and back and front facings, will require 6 ft. of material, 11 in. by

¾ in., and the inside blocks about 2 ft. of ¾ in. by ¾ in. All these thicknesses are for finished stuff, and should, with the exception of the pin-blocks and belly, be of the best yellow deal or pine. The latter is the most expensive, but the result is generally much more satisfactory, both in tone and lightness. A piece of veneer, a few feet of moulding, and one or two more pieces of wood, which will be mentioned later, will complete the list of requirements.

Begin by getting out the blocks. Take the piece of oak, or beech, 3½ in. by 3 in., and, having squared its surfaces, gauge a line one inch from the edge on the

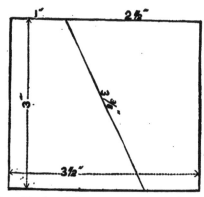

Fig. 161.—Cutting Wrest-pin and Hitch-pin Blocks.

3½ in. face. Then turn it over and gauge another line on the opposite face, at the same distance from the edge. Draw a line at each end of the block from one gauge mark to the other, and divide the block down its whole length on these gauge marks. The result will be two blocks with sloping faces 3⅜ in. wide (Fig. 161). Clean these faces up and gauge a mark ¼ in. from the top edge on the 2½ in. face; plane down square to this mark, and this will reduce the sloping face to 2⅞ in. In the flat thus formed shoot a half-round groove ⅛ in. deep and ⅛ in. from the edge A (Fig. 162), and at a distance of ½ in. from the top edge shoot another groove B, ¼ in deep and ₁₆³ in. wide. The block should now be similar to Fig. 162, and, to give it a finish, it should be rounded off at the corner c, as shown by the dotted line.

Of the two grooves, that on the top is intended for

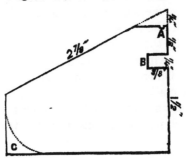

Fig. 162.—Section of Block with Groove.

the pressure-bar over which the strings pass, and the one in the side is to receive the edge of the belly.

Another and simpler plan is to do without this latter groove, and in place thereof glue and nail a fillet ⅞ in. by ⅜ in. thick to the block so that its top edge is ¾ in. below the top edge of the block (Fig. 163). On this fillet the edge of the belly will rest, and, if built this way, the fillet need not be put on till the shell is quite finished and ready for the belly.

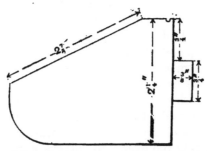

Fig. 163—Section of Block with Fillet for Dulcimer Belly.

The blocks now being ready, proceed with the back. Cut off 2 ft. 6 in. of the 9-in. stuff, and another piece of the same 1 ft. 9 in. long. Shoot one edge of each for

joining, and reduce the shorter piece to 7 in. in width.
Draw a line across the centre of each, and join up so
that the lines come level. When thoroughly dry, cut
and plane it to measure 2 ft. 4 in. on the lower edge,
1 ft. 1½ in. on the upper, and 1 ft. 2 in. from front to
back. If half these distances are measured from the
centre line, it will ensure each side being cut to the
same angle. Gauge a mark on the underside of the
blocks 2 in. from the inner edge, and screw the back on,
level with these marks, with No. 6 screws, 1¼ in. long, at
intervals of 2 in., beginning at 2 in. from the front

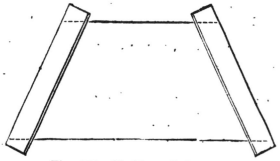

Fig. 164.—Marking off Corners.

edge. Grease the screws with tallow before turning
them in, as they must come out again before finally
fixing on the back. Cut off the projecting ends of the
blocks at top and bottom, and plane them off square and
level, as shown at Fig. 164 by the dotted lines.

Take the back off again, and lay the screws in
readiness. Clean off all chips and burrs that may
have been raised ; take some hot and strong, but not
thick, glue, and, having well warmed the parts to be
joined, quickly run over 2 in. of the edge of the back
and the underside of the block, and, slipping them
together, work them up and down a few times to get a
good connection. Screw up properly, clean off the
glue that has squeezed out, and repeat the operation on
the other block. Fit three blocks ¾ in. square by 3½ in.

long accurately into the angles formed by the pin-
blocks and the back, the first one at a distance of 2 in.
from the bottom edge (A, Fig. 165). Then clean off and
set aside for a day or two to dry.

The instrument, which is now beginning to take
shape, has yet to be strengthened by braces at the
back and front. For the latter, cut a mortise in the
front end of each block 1½ in. long, 1 in. wide, and ⅜ in.
deep, at D (Fig. 165). Take a piece of ⅝-in. stuff of the
required length, and cut it to fit accurately into each
mortise, and, at the same time, fit perfectly level on
the back. The top edge of this brace at each end must

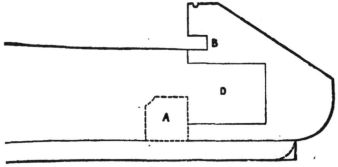

Fig. 165.—Fitting Blocks into Angles of Back.

be level with the lower edge of the groove B (Fig.
165), or the top of the fillet if that is used instead. It
must not, however, be quite straight from block to
block, but should have a rise of ½ in. in the centre, thus
presenting a slightly arched top. This will give a
convex surface to the belly, this being found to give
a better tone and to present a greater resistance to the
downward pressure of the strings. When the brace is
finished, bore a hole through each tenon to take a 2-in.
cut clasp. Fit it into its place, and bore a series of holes
through the back into the brace (about eight will be
sufficient) to take 1½-in. wire nails or brads. Take the
brace out again, and, after warming the parts, quickly
glue tenons and the bottom edge of the brace, also

J

the mortises. Whipping the brace into its place, drive the nails home, and punch the heads in. The back brace is made and fitted in exactly the same way, except that no curve or rise is given to the top edge. It is better to clean off all superfluous glue at once. This is best done by first scraping off the thickest and then washing with very hot water and a rag or sponge. If any glue is allowed to remain on, it may afterwards cause a great deal of trouble by cracking or warping off.

The inner bridges require attention next. These are necessary to support the belly, which, without them, would not bear the pressure of the strings, but would most likely swamp or pucker, if it did not split. They also act the part of the sound-post in the violin, by connecting back and front together. For the treble bridge,

Fig. 166.—Side View of Inner Bridges.

take a piece of the ½-in. stuff, 2 in. wide, and fit it between the front and back braces at a distance of 10 in. from the bottom left-hand corner and 4 in. from the top corner. It should be let into the braces about ⅛ in., and planed off flush with the tops of them. The bass bridge is fitted in exactly the same way, 3 in. from and parallel to the right-hand block. These bridges must be considerably lightened by boring a series of holes through them with a ¾-in. centre-bit. After the bridges are fitted, and before finally fixing them, take them out, draw a line down the centre on each side, and mark it off at intervals of 1½ in. Bore on these marks till the bit is just beginning to come through, then reverse and complete the boring from the other side (Fig. 166). Glue them in, and fasten them from the back with two screws each, the holes for which should have been bored previously.

The shell should now present the appearance shown

in Fig. 167, in which A is the wrest-pin block ; B, hitch-pin block ; c, front brace ; D, back brace ; E, treble bridge ; F, bass bridge.

Now proceed to the fitting of the sound-board. First draw a line down each block, ¼ in. from the inner edge, which line will correspond to the depth of the grooves. Cut the sound-board to these marks, and clean up the edges to fit easily in the grooves by sliding it up from the front. It will, perhaps, be a little difficult to do this owing to the arched top of the front brace, but a little gentle persuasion and tapping will accomplish it. It is

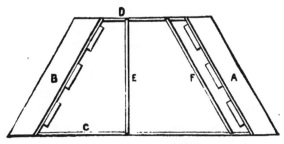

Fig. 167.—Shell of Dulcimer.

not necessary to have it fit tightly, but only tight enough to prevent rattling.

Having fitted it, and reduced it to within ¼ in. of the width it will require to be when finished, mark the position of the sound-holes. For the treble, make a dot, 7 in. from the bottom and 4½ in. from the left block, and 6 in. to the right of this make another dot for the centre of the bass sound-hole. Take the board out again and cut out these holes 2½ in. in diameter, either with a pair of cutting compasses, a cutting-out bit, or a fine-toothed pad-saw. If the latter is used care must be taken not to splinter the edges. The belly must now be thoroughly sand-papered on both sides, and will then be ready for fixing. Glue the edges and slip it up into the grooves and then fasten it down to the front and back braces with ¾-in. brads. If the second plan of fillets instead of

grooves is adopted, it will only be necessary to cut the
board to fit accurately and nail it down all round after,
of course, having cut the sound-holes.   The belly being
now fixed, plane off the back and front edges level with
the braces, clean off also any inequalities that may show

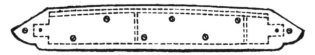

Fig. 168.—Front of Dulcimer with Facing on.

themselves, and then the facings may be put on.   They
are made of ⅜-in. stuff, fitted over the braces and glued
and screwed on, thus forming an additional support.
The top edges should be raised the same distance above
the level of the belly that the blocks stand at, thus
forming a rebate of the same depth all round ; and the
ends are shaped to the ends of the blocks.   Fig. 168
shows the front of the instrument with facing on, under
which the dotted lines show the outlines of the belly,
brace, and inner bridges.

The veneering may now be attempted.   Take a strip
of walnut, mahogany, or any other suitable veneer, and
cut it to about ¼ in. wider than the facing.   Having
gone over the latter with a toothing plane, first noting
that all screws, etc., are well below the surface, glue on
with the best glue.   When dry, clean down level with the
edges of the facings, take another strip of the same width
as the top of the facing, and cut it to fit exactly between

Fig. 169.—Full-size Wrest-pin.

the blocks,   A short piece will serve for each end of the
blocks, and will hide the joint between the block and the
facing, and give a neat finish,   When quite dry, the
edges may be filed and sand-papered off, and the whole
gone over with a scraper.

A most important and, at the same time, most difficult part of the work has now to be done, namely, the setting out of the blocks for wrest-pins (Fig. 169) and hitch-pins. Four lines, at distances of $\frac{1}{2}$ in. from each other, are drawn down the centre portion of each block from top to bottom, and on the front or inner line of the right-hand block make a dot at a distance of $1\frac{1}{2}$ in. from the front inner edge. Another dot must be made on the same line 2 in. from the back, and the distance between these two dots divided into nineteen spaces, thus making twenty dots in all. Go to No. 2 line, and, starting $\frac{1}{8}$ in. higher up, divide that line in the same way as No. 1, after which lines 3 and 4 may be proceeded with. The hitch-pin block is set out in the same

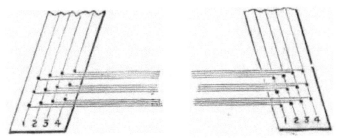

Fig. 170.—Setting out Dulcimer Hitch-pin Block.

manner, except that the first or lowest string comes on the outside line. Reference to Fig. 170 will explain this. By this method the four strings of each note are made of the same length, thus ensuring equal tension.

The polishing or varnishing of the instrument is now begun. Polishing is decidedly the best, as it lasts longer, gives an altogether better appearance, and does not clog the tone so much as varnishing is apt to do. If, however, it is to be varnished, first go over all the parts carefully with the finest glass-paper, and then stain the belly with ebony stain, taking care not to come above the level of the blocks. Stain the back also inside, as far as can be reached through the sound-holes, and the backs of the blocks, and for about an inch all

round the back itself. When dry, if the colour is
satisfactory, coat it all over with size made of glue 1
part, and warm water 5 parts. This being firmly set,
varnish with the best copal varnish, which must be very
lightly and evenly applied, and then the instrument may
be set aside in a place free from dust for the varnish to
get thoroughly dry and hard. In the meantime, get
ready the wrest-pins, hitch-pins, bridges, etc., necessary
to complete the job. Time and trouble may be saved
by getting these fittings ready-made.

Eighty wrest-pins will be required, and the same
number of hitch-pins. For the wrest-pins (Fig. 169), get
a piece of iron wire about 12 ft. long and No. 6 size
B.W.G. (Birmingham wire gauge). Cut it into lengths

Fig. 171.—Full-size Bridge for Dulcimer.

of 1¾ in. either with a hard chisel and hammer, a hack
saw, or the edge of a half-round file ; round up both ends
of these lengths and flatten one end on both sides for
½ in. down, either by filing or hammering. At the bottom
of the flat part thus formed, drill a small hole to receive
the end of the string. The part below the hole should
be slightly roughened with a course file. Thread these
pins on a piece of wire stretched between two points,
and black them for about half their length with
Brunswick or Berlin black. When dry they will be
ready for use.

The ornaments for the sound-holes may consist of
plain rings, or they may be of fretwork, inlaid stars,
or other designs. They must fit the sound-hole

tightly, and be firmly glued in after the varnishing
or polishing is done.

The bridges (Fig. 171) are made of beech or other
hard wood, turned to the pattern shown, and chiselled
off to the shape as per dotted lines. On the edge
thus formed a groove is filed, in which rests a piece
of brass wire over which the strings pass. The bottoms
of the bridges should be turned rather hollow. They
may be varnished in the natural colour, or, if preferred,
they may be bronzed or gilded.

The feet are four flat balls, 1 in. in diameter and
¾ in. thick, and are screwed on, one at each corner

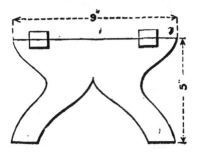

Fig. 172.—Dulcimer Stand.

of the back, after it has been covered with blue or
other coloured paper.

The stand is made of ¾-in. stuff veneered on both
sides diagonally, so that the grain of one side
crosses that of the other, to give additional strength.
It is 9 in. long and 5 in. high, and may be of any
fancy pattern. That usually adopted is shown at
Fig. 172. It is screwed on to the back with a pair
of 1-in. butts at a distance of 2 in. from the back
edge.

The pressure-bars are two pieces of brass wire ⅛ in. in
diameter, cut to the exact length of the grooves in
the blocks, in which they fit. They should have the
ends rounded and be well polished.

The wrest-pin block may now be bored. The No. 6

wire, of which the pins are made, measures $\frac{5}{16}$ in. in
diameter ; consequently the holes must be considerably
smaller than this, or the pins, owing to the "draught"
of the strings, and the turning up and down necessary,
would soon work loose and the pitch run down. Take,
therefore, a $\frac{3}{32}$-in. spoon-bit, or, better still, a twist drill,
and on it fit tightly a "stop," which leaves exactly 1 in.
of the bit exposed for boring. This stop, which may be
made of a piece of metal tube, is necessary to regulate
the depth of the holes. Begin by boring the lowest
hole, keeping the bit at angles to the face of the block.
When that is bored, insert therein a piece of wood
like a pencil and about 3 in. long. It should just fit,

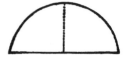

Fig. 173.—Making Moulding Round Dulcimer Belly.

and as it is intended to act as a guide for the boring
of the succeeding holes, it should be shifted from time
to time. When all the holes are bored, they should
be slightly countersunk. The borings carefully removed, the pins can then be put in by turning them
with the tuning key, not by hammering. An
expeditious way of turning the pins in is to remove
the tuning key from the handle and fit it to the
brace.

The hitch-pins, which are made of iron or brass
wire, $\frac{3}{32}$ in. in diameter, are $\frac{3}{4}$ in. long and pointed at
one end. A hole is bored about $\frac{1}{4}$ in. into the block with
a small bradawl, and the pin is then driven in till $\frac{1}{4}$ in.
remains. When all are inserted, take a good-sized
flat file and go over the tops till they are level.
All that now remains to be done, previous to stringing
up, is the ornamentation of the sound-board and the
fitting of the moulding round it. The plainer this is
the better, as elaborate patterns only harbour dust and
are difficult to keep clean. The best kind to use is

one that is made by taking a piece of $\frac{3}{8}$ in. by $\frac{1}{4}$ in. pine or mahogany and making a half-round bead of it, which is then divided lengthwise and the sawn edges planed. This makes a quarter-circle moulding (Fig. 173), which, when nailed in its place, just comes below the edges of the block and facings. It should be polished or gilded before fixing, and may be fastened in with brass pins. Care must be taken that the mitres fit accurately, as nothing looks worse than a gaping corner. Be careful that the varnish on the sound-board is quite dry, or the gold leaf or bronze will certainly stick where not wanted.

The stringing of the instrument may now be proceeded with. For this purpose, 2 oz. of No. 9 and 1 oz. of No. 8 brass, and 2 oz. of No. 8 and 1 oz. of No. 7 steel music wire will be required. This is measured with a special

Fig. 174.—Eye for Dulcimer String.

gauge called the M.W.G. (music wire gauge). If the pins are not drilled, the strings may be fastened in the following manner : Take a piece of strong black thread and knot the ends together so as to form a loop 2 in. long ; pass this round the pin, thread the knotted end through the loop, and, when the pin is turned to the right, it will draw up tight and gather round it. Make a small hook at the end of the wire and insert it in the free end of the loop, and it will be found sufficiently strong for the purpose.

Cut off twenty pieces of No. 18 B.W.G. brass wire to fit the tops of the bridges, and fasten a strip of velvet ribbon or scarlet cloth on each block between the inside pins and the grooves. Having laid the pressure-bars in their places, take the coil of No. 9 brass wire in the left hand and unwind sufficient for one string. In the end of this twist an eye, $\frac{1}{2}$ in. long, and finish it off

by turning the free end of the wire twice round the
string, after which the end may be cut off, leaving a tail
at right angles ¼ in. long (Fig. 174). Put this eye on the
hitch-pin, cut off the string 6 in. beyond the corresponding wrest-pin, and insert the end in the hole or loop.
If the pegs are drilled, do not let the wire come through,
but only level. Turn the pin to the right and see that
the string gathers evenly and regularly round it, as in
Fig. 175, and not irregularly as in Fig. 176. Arrange so
that each succeeding string lies on the tail of the one preceding it ; and, when a note is complete, place under it a
bridge with a piece of wire on top. String the first five
bass notes with No. 9 and the remainder with No. 8 brass.
Get all the brass strings on first, and be careful not to
put any of them on the pegs intended for the steel. The
steel strings are put on in precisely the same manner,
and the bridges under them stand about 2 in. to the left
of the centre. The bridges under the brass strings stand
2½ in. from, and parallel to, the block.

Another kind of eye, and one that has the merit of
being very simple and effective, is made by placing a
piece of wire, a size or two larger than the hitch-pin,
upright in the vice (or it may be driven into the bench),
and round this the wire is carried twice and the tail
finished in the same manner as in the previous method.
This is really a slip-eye, as, when the string is tightened
up, the part forming the tail slips down to the hitch-pin
and is there held securely.

Still-another plan of stringing, in which the eye is
dispensed with altogether, is as follows : Insert the
wire in No. 1 wrest-pin, and, having wound on sufficient,
carry it across to the corresponding hitch-pin, round
which take a whole turn to the right ; then go to No. 2
hitch-pin, and round that take a whole turn to the left ;
then carry across to No. 2 wrest-pin, cut off, and wind.
By this method the stringing can be accomplished in
about half the time taken by the other.

In tuning, the notes should first be "roughed up"
gradually to the scale, as shown at Fig. 177, and when

they are beginning to stand, get the treble bridges into their correct places. The first, second, third, and fourth bridges divide their respective strings into intervals of a " fifth " each, which means that the left portion is seven semitones higher than the right ; the fifth and sixth intervals are eight semitones, the seventh is seven, the eighth is six, the ninth is five, and the tenth is three. This method gives a chromatic scale from the lower E, the sixth brass note, the remaining notes below that being diatonic. The brass notes are tuned thus : The

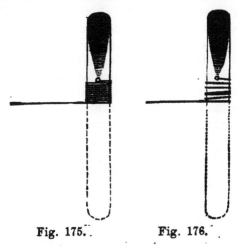

Fig. 175. Fig. 176.

Fig. 175.—Properly Wound Pin. Fig. 176.—Badly Wound Pin.

first, second, third, and fourth are octaves below the steel notes next above them ; the fifth, sixth, and seventh are octaves below the first, second, and third steel on the left of the bridges ; and the eighth, ninth, and tenth are octaves below the steel notes preceding them. A little study of the diagram (Fig. 177) will soon give a good idea of the foregoing arrangement. This scale will hold good for all instruments of twenty bridges, as, no matter what the size may be, the lowest note is always called G, although its pitch may be any other. The best method of tuning is to take a stout piece of quill in the left hand and chip each string as it is tuned.

The beaters are made of cane or whalebone, generally the former. Take a piece of stoutish cane 15 in. in length, about ½ in. in diameter, free from joints if possible, and split it in four, lengthwise ; or take two pieces of the same length and about ₁³₆ in. diameter (these make by far the best beaters), and taper them along their whole length by planing or otherwise till the thin ends will easily curl. Form these into oval rings 1½ in. long. Fasten them with thread that has been well waxed with cobbler's wax, smooth the shanks up with glass-paper, and then bind the lower and front parts of the bows with two or three layers of Berlin wool. Continue it for about an inch along the shanks, fasten off with thread, and cut each to a length of 11 in. from bow to butt.

When playing the dulcimer it should be placed on a table without a cover, and raised at the back by means of the stand provided for that purpose ; the performer should then take his place opposite the centre, and on a seat which is just high enough to bring his elbows on a level with the front edge of the sound-board, and at such a distance from it that he can easily reach the top notes without bending the body forward. The arms should be kept close to but not touching the sides, and the beaters should be held firmly but lightly between the thumbs and first and second fingers of each hand. The blow should be given from the wrist, not the fore-arm, and should partake more of the character of a "flick" than a downright blow. This lightness and flexibility of wrist is only to be acquired by practice, and for this purpose the best of all exercises are the scales, which should be persevered in till they can be run up and down with the greatest facility. The correct way of playing the scale is to strike two succeeding notes with each hand as often as it is found possible to do so. Thus the scale of G would be played G A left, B C right, D E left, F G right, and so on to the top, returning in the same order. When the scales can be played without making a mistake, or

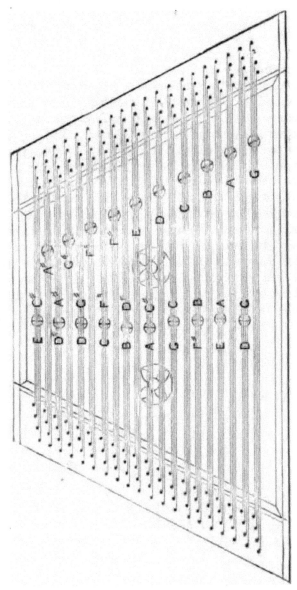

Fig. 177.—Scale and Approximate Position of Dulcimer Bridges.

striking two notes at once, simple airs may be attempted, but on no account should "scraps" be indulged in.

A dulcimer should be carefully protected from damp, which would quickly ruin it. For this purpose a wood case is the best, and it also makes a most excellent resonator to stand the instrument on when playing. The sides and ends should be of ⅜-in. stuff, with ⅜ in. for back and lid. The joints in these two latter should be grooved and tongued, and the ends at the back should project ½ in. to form feet to stand upon. The case should be lined with baize, and furnished with a good strap or an iron drop-handle for convenience of carrying. It should also be well painted, of course, before lining it. It ought to be 2 in. wider at the back than the dulcimer itself, to allow room to insert the fingers to take the instrument out. Always keep an old silk handkerchief or soft duster in the case, and never put the dulcimer after using without first wiping the strings and taking the dust off the sound-board. Above all, do not let it get out of tune or allow the pitch to drop. Constant tuning is necessary to keep the dulcimer perfectly in order.

INDEX.

Amber Oil Varnish, 67—68
American Banjo, Head of, 110
—— Guitar, 92
—— Mandoline, 90
Andalusian Guitar, 92
Arion Zither, 133—134
Banjo, 99—116
—— Bowl, 99—102
—— Bridge, 106
——, Diameter of, 115
—— Head, 110
—— ——, American Method of
    Putting on, 110
——, Parchment used for, 104—106
——, Piccolo, 106—110
——, ——, Bowl of, 107
——, ——, Handle of, 106
——, Six-string, 99—116
—— Tail-piece, 106
Beaters, Dulcimer, 155—156
Bending Violin Ribs, 43—45
Callipers, 19
Compasses, 17
Concert Zither, 117
Cramps, Iron, 15—16
Cremonese Violins, 9
Cutting Gauge, 17
Dividers, Spring 17
Double Bass Violin, 71—73
Dulcimer, 141—158
—— Back, 143—144
—— Beaters, 155—156
—— Belly, 147—148
—— Blocks, Setting out, 142—143
—— ——, Setting out, for Wrest-
    pins, 149
—— Braces for Strengthening,
    145, 146
—— Bridges, 146—151
—— Feet, 151
—— Hitch-pin Block, Setting
    out, 149
—— Hitch-pins, 152
——, Polishing, 149
—— Sound-board, 147
—— Sound-holes, Ornaments
    for, 150
—— Stand, 151

Dulcimer, Stringing, 155
——, Tools for Making, 141
—— Tuning, 154—155
——, Veneering, 148
——, Wood for, 141
—— Wrest-pin Block, Boring,
    151—152
—— —— ——, Setting out, 149
——, Wrest-pins for, 149
Elégie Zither, 117
Flat-backed Mandoline, 82—91
French Guitar, 92
Frets in Zither, Fastening, 126
Gauge, Cutting, 17
—— Register, 19
——, Thicknessing, 18—19
Gouges, 7—18
Guitar, 92—98
——, American, 92
——, Andalusian, 92
—— Belly, 92
—— Bridge, 96
—— Finger-board, 97
——, French, 92
—— Mould, Marking, 95
——, Spanish, 92
——, Spanish Lyre, 92
Harp, Prince of Wales', 138—139
—— Zither, 134—135
Hitch-pin Block, Setting out, for
    Dulcimer, 149
Hitch-pins, Dulcimer, 152
——, Zither, 123—129
Inside Moulds for Violins, 39—40
Japanese Violin, 77
—— —— with Hexagonal Body,
    77
Lyre-guitar, Spanish, 92
Mandoline, 82—89
——, American, 90
—— Back and Belly, 85
—— Bridge, 88
—— Finger-board, 88
——, Flat-backed, 82—91
—— Handle, 82—85
—— Machine Head, 90
—— Tail-piece, 89—90
Mould (see Violin Mould)

Oil Varnishes, 68
Outside Moulds for Violins, 30
Parchment Head of Banjo, 101—10;
Philomela Zither, 135 -137
Piccolo Banjo, 106—110
——— Bowl, 107
——— —— Handle, 106
Planes, Thumb, 24—27
Plectrum, 139—140
Prince of Wales' Harp, 138—139
Purfling gauge, 27—29
—— Knife, 29
—— Picker, 29
—— Waist of Violin, 48—49
Scrapers, Steel. 27
Screws, Hand, 16
——, Wood-carvers', 16
Sounding Table for Zither, 139
Spanish Guitar, 92
—— Lyre-guitar, 92
Spring Dividers, 17
Square, 17
Staining Violin, 66
Steel Scrapers, 27
Stradivarius Violin, 9
—— —— Mould, 39
Streich Zither, 117—135—136
Stringing Dulcimer, 155
Strings for Zither, 129—131—132
Table, Sounding, 139
Testing Violin Moulds, 37
Thicknessing, 19—23
—— Gauge, 18—19
Thumb Planes, 24—27
Tools for Making Violins, 15—29
Tuning Dulcimer, 154—155
—— Zither, 132
Varnish, Amber, 67
——, Oil, 68
——, Removing, 68
—— for Violins, 66
Varnishing Violin, 64-70
Viennese Method of Stringing Zither, 129—133
Viola, Zither. 134—135
Violin, Aged Appearance to, 69
—— Back, "Trueing up," 42
—— ——, Wood for, 10
—— Bass-bar, 12—56
—— Belly. 54—55
—— ——, Wood or, 10
—— Bridge, Fitting, 69
——, Cremonese, 9
—— Double Bass (see Double Bass Violin)
—— Finger-board, 62
——, Glue for, 13
——, Japanese (see Japanese)
—— Making, 41—63

Violin, Materials for Making, 9 - 29
—— Moulds, 30—40
—— ——, Inside, 39—40
—— ——, Outside, 30
—— ——, Stradivarius, 39
—— ——, Testing, 37
—— Neck, 58 - 62
—— Peg Holes, Cutting, 62
—— Purfling, 12—15
—— ——, Waist of, 48—49
—— Rib Strips, Bending, 42—43
—— Ribs, Attaching to Back, 50—51
—— ——, Bending, 14—43—45
—— ——, Fixing, 57
—— Scroll, 58—62
—— ——, Carving, 10—11
—— Sound-holes, 54
—— Sound-post, 12—70
——, Stradivarius, 9—41
——, Staining, 66
——, Tools for Making, 15—29
—— Varnish, 66
—— ——, Removing, 68
——, Varnishing, 64—70
Violoncello, 74—76
—— Bass-bar, 75—76
—— Bridge, 75
——, Wood for, 75
Waist of Violin, Purfling, 48—49
Wood for Violins, 10—11
Wood-carvers' Screws, 16
Zither, 117—140
——, Arion, 133—134
—— Bridge, 125
——, Case for, 139
——, Concert, 117
——, Elégie, 117
——, Fastening Frets in, 126
—— Finger-board, 126—128
——, Harp, 134—135
——, Inserting Hitch-pins in, 128—129
——, Philomela, 135—137
——, Plectrum, 139—140
——, Prince of Wales' Harp, 133—139
—— Ribs, 122
——, Sounding Table for. 139
——, Streich, 117—145—136
——, Stringing, 129
—— Strings, Choice of, 131—132
—— ——, Cost of, 129
——, Stuttgart Method of Stringing, 129
——, Tuning, 132
——, Viennese Method of Stringing, 129—133
Zither Viola, 134—135

HANDICRAFT SERIES (*continued*).

Electro-Plating. With Numerous Engravings and Diagrams.
Contents.—Introduction. Tanks, Vats, and other Apparatus. Batteries, Dynamos, and Electrical Accessories. Appliances for Preparing and Finishing Work. Silver-Plating, Copper-Plating. Gold-Plating. Nickel-Plating and Cycle-Plating. Finishing Electro-Plated Goods. Electro-Plating with Various Metals and Alloys. Index.

Clay Modelling and Plaster Casting. With 153 Engravings and Diagrams.
Contents.—Introduction. Drawing for Modellers. Tools and Material for Modelling. Clay Modelling. Modelling Ornament. Modelling the Human Figure. Waste-moulding Process for Plaster Casting. Piece-moulding and Gelatine Moulding. Taking Casts from Nature. Clay Squeezing or Clay Moulding. Finishing Plaster Casts. Picture Frame in Plaster. Index.

Violins and Other Stringed Instruments. With about 180 Illustrations.
Contents.—Materials and Tools for Violin Making. Violin Moulds. Violin Making. Varnishing and Finishing Violins. Double Bass and a Violoncello. Japanese One-string Violin. Mandolin Making. Guitar Making. Banjo Making. Zither-Making. Dulcimer Making. Index.

Glass Writing, Embossing, and Fascia Work. (Including the Making and Fixing of Wood Letters and Illuminated Signs.) With 129 Illustrations.
Contents.—Plain Lettering and Simple Tablets. Gold Lettering. Blocked Letters. Stencil Cutting. Gold Etching. Embossing. French or Treble Embossing. Incised Fascias, Stall-plates, and Grained Background. Letters in Perspective; Spacing Letters. Arrangement of Wording and Colors. Wood Letters. Illuminated Signs. Temporary Signs for Windows. Imitation Inlaid Signs. Imitation Mosaic Signs. Specimen Alphabets. Index.

Other Volumes in Preparation.